# Psychic Development

*An Essential Guide to Telepathy, Divination, Astral Projection, Mediumship, Clairvoyance, Healing, and Psychic Witchcraft*

© Copyright 2021

This book's contents may not be reproduced, duplicated or transmitted without direct written permission from the author.

Under no circumstances will any legal responsibility or blame be held against the publisher for any reparation, damages, or monetary loss due to the information herein, either directly or indirectly.

Legal Notice:

You cannot amend, distribute, sell, use, quote, or paraphrase any part of the content within this book without the author's consent.

Disclaimer Notice:

Please note the information contained within this document is for educational and entertainment purposes only. No warranties of any kind are expressed or implied. Readers acknowledge that the author is not engaging in the rendering of legal, financial, medical, or professional advice. Please consult a licensed professional before attempting any techniques outlined in this book.

By reading this document, the reader agrees that under no circumstances is the author responsible for any losses, direct or indirect, which are incurred as a result of the use of the information contained within this document, including, but not limited to, errors, omissions, or inaccuracies.

## Your Free Gift (only available for a limited time)

Thanks for getting this book! If you want to learn more about various spirituality topics, then join Mari Silva's community and get a free guided meditation MP3 for awakening your third eye. This guided meditation mp3 is designed to open and strengthen ones third eye so you can experience a higher state of consciousness. Simply visit the link below the image to get started.

https://spiritualityspot.com/meditation

# Contents

INTRODUCTION ................................................................................1
CHAPTER ONE: ARE YOU READY TO BECOME A PSYCHIC? .................3
CHAPTER TWO: HOW TO TAP INTO YOUR INHERENT PSYCHIC ABILITIES ........................................................................................12
    Meditation ................................................................................ 17
    Spirit Guides ............................................................................ 19
    Psychometry ............................................................................ 21
CHAPTER THREE: PSYCHIC TOOLS ................................................24
    Pendulum ................................................................................ 25
    Tarot Cards ............................................................................. 27
    Crystals .................................................................................... 30
    Runes ....................................................................................... 32
    Astrology ................................................................................. 33
CHAPTER FOUR: UNDERSTAND THE ASTRAL BODY .........................35
    What are the Seven Chakras? ................................................. 37
    Technique 1: Run Energy Through the Chakras ................... 41
    Technique 2: Visualize to Release Negative Energy ............. 44
CHAPTER FIVE: ASTRAL TRAVEL ...................................................47
    The Monroe Institute Technique ............................................ 52
    Lucid Dreams .......................................................................... 55
CHAPTER SIX: BEGIN YOUR MEDIUMSHIP .....................................57

How to Tune Into the Spirit World .................................................................. 61
**CHAPTER SEVEN: UNLOCK TELEPATHY** ............................................ **64**
　Exercises to Develop Telepathic Abilities ............................................... 68
**CHAPTER EIGHT: TYPES OF DIVINATION** ........................................ **72**
　Scrying ........................................................................................................ 75
　Tea Leaves Reading ................................................................................ 75
　Sand Divination ........................................................................................ 75
　Pyromancy .................................................................................................. 76
　Osteomancy ................................................................................................ 76
　Numerology ................................................................................................ 76
　Automatic Writing .................................................................................... 76
**CHAPTER NINE: PRACTICE DIVINATION** ........................................ **78**
**CHAPTER TEN: THE POWER OF CLAIRVOYANCE** ....................... **83**
**CHAPTER ELEVEN: SPIRITUAL HEALING: WORK WITH ENERGY** .............................................................................................................. **87**
　Reiki Healing ............................................................................................. 89
　Qigong ......................................................................................................... 91
　Pranic Healing .......................................................................................... 93
　Quantum Healing .................................................................................... 96
**CHAPTER TWELVE: CRYSTALS FOR HEALING AND PERSONAL POWER** ................................................................................................................. **98**
**CONCLUSION** ............................................................................................... **102**
**HERE'S ANOTHER BOOK BY MARI SILVA THAT YOU MIGHT LIKE** ...................................................................................................................... **103**
**YOUR FREE GIFT (ONLY AVAILABLE FOR A LIMITED TIME)** ........... **104**
**REFERENCES** ................................................................................................ **105**

# Introduction

If you were told right now that you have special psychic abilities that border on the supernatural, you'd likely laugh hysterically. Well, that is, if you are not yet familiar with psychic development. Do you just presume that you are a regular Joe with nothing special going on? Well, you are far from being ordinary. You have a lot of things going on for you, but you have yet to realize it. No, this does not mean you are unusual or different from others. If you were to call everyone "special" based on psychic powers, everyone would be exceptional in one way or another. Why? Because everyone, including you, has psychic abilities.

Since you are new to psychic abilities and powers, your perception of psychic gifts might be based on what you have seen on the TV over the years. As a result, you may have grown up believing that psychic abilities are only accessible to a handful of people who you presume to be unusual or extraordinary. Well, whatever you learned about psychics and mediums from the TV is a fluke, or at least most of it is. Everyone has psychic abilities. Some people may be more predisposed to these abilities than others. That means that certain people may be better than others with their psychic powers, but in the end, everyone has psychic abilities.

The problem lies in recognizing your psychic ability and learning how to use that ability to improve every aspect of your life; I aim to help you understand that. The process needed to discover your psychic power and awaken your psychic senses is called *psychic development*. Psychic development is a journey of awakening that involves realizing your true capabilities as a human. The purpose of this book is simple: It serves as your guide through your psychic development journey, taking you step-by-step through your psychic awakening process.

Written in clear and concise language, this book caters to anybody from beginners to those with basic knowledge of the psychic development process. So, it does not matter whether you are just learning about psychic abilities or know the basics this book is for you. From the first chapter to the last, I give an in-depth breakdown of different psychic abilities and how you can hone them. There are simple and straightforward exercises, techniques, and examples to aid your understanding of the topic to make it easier for you. What makes this book different from similar books on the market is that it has up-to-date and easy-to-understand information. More importantly, the exercises, techniques, and instructions are hands-on, meaning you can put them to practice at any time.

If you want a book with a healthy mix of theory and practical instructions to help you unlock your psychic gifts, this is the book for you. Without further delay, let's start your journey!

# Chapter One: Are You Ready to Become a Psychic?

Regardless of how you feel about psychics and psychic abilities, you also have psychic powers – to a certain extent. As I said in the introduction, everyone possesses psychic abilities. Many have learned to hone and use their abilities, while others leave their abilities dormant, waiting for them to be awakened. If you have ever used your intuition or "gut feelings" to make a decision that turned out to be right, you are undoubtedly psychic. This begs the question, "Is having intuition the same as being psychic?"

To some degree, yes. Being intuitive is the same as being psychic, but psychic abilities can be honed to go beyond just intuition. This means you can train yourself to improve your psychic powers beyond the power of your intuition alone. Rather than relying on your gut feeling to make a decision, you can hone your psychic senses to where you just know what to do or what not to do. It can be that easy. But the process of learning is not an easy one.

Many people begin their psychic awakening journey, believing it will be a simple and straightforward one, but they often become disappointed. The disappointment stems from their going on the journey, thinking they can achieve a lot within a couple of months. In fact, I met someone who called psychic abilities a fad because they couldn't achieve astral projection a week after they began learning. I was dismayed to know that a supposed psychic made them believe that they could learn astral projection in five days if they practiced consistently. Consistency may be vital in developing psychic abilities. Still, it won't help you understand any of the skills in a few days.

When one begins their psychic learning, the best thing is to think of it as learning a new skill. You probably would not know everything about a skill such as graphic designing in five days. So, why would you expect to learn clairvoyance or telepathy in five days? Just as you would need to advance in any skill you learn by continually learning new techniques and methods, you need to do the same with psychic development. This means you must be patient, enduring, and open to advances in learning. Before you answer the question, "Am I ready to become a psychic?" you must make sure that you will be patient throughout the journey. Patience is single-handedly the most critical element in developing psychic abilities. Unless you are patient, you likely won't last more than a few weeks before you give up on honing your psychic skills.

You must understand that people learn at different paces. Some learn faster than others. If you begin your psychic learning with a friend today, you won't both learn at the same rate. Your friend may have become good at seeing auras with colors before you even start seeing just a faint light. If this happens, it does not mean you also won't get to that point. It merely means they are a faster learner than you, which is fine. You need to work at your own pace, not theirs. So, it shouldn't matter what someone else is achieving. You only need to focus on your progress because that is all that matters. Once you understand these simple facts, it is safe to say that you are ready to become a psychic. But really, *what is a psychic?*

The simplest way to define a psychic is to think of a person with extrasensory perception. The key phrase here is "extrasensory perception," which can acquire information without using the recognized sensory channels. To put it simply, someone with extrasensory perception can obtain information without using their normal senses of sight, hearing, touch, smell, or taste. If you have extrasensory perception, you can see things that your ordinary eyes cannot see. Extrasensory perception is the basis of any psychic abilities, including clairvoyance, telepathy, mediumship, etc. As a psychic, you can see, hear, sense, feel, or taste beyond the limitations of the material world.

Throughout history, there have been documented and undocumented reports of "special" people who could solve different problems in multifarious aspects of life, from business to relationships. There are examples and instances of people using clairvoyance, mediumship, precognition, and other psychic abilities in cultures worldwide.

In Ancient India, sages were masters in the art of clairvoyance. One such example of an Ancient Indian philosopher using clairvoyance is the story of Sanjay, an assistant to Dhritrashtra, the father of Kauravas. During Mahabharata's war between Pandavas and Kauravas, Sanjay relayed everything happening on the battlefield to Dhritrashtra, who was blind. He did this even though he was thousands of miles away from the venue of the battle. Everyone believed that Sanjay had the gift of the psychic eye. In other words, he had the gift of clairvoyance.

Even in Europe, there are stories of known psychics such as Edgar Cayce, an American psychic famous for his clairvoyant abilities. Cayce was regarded as a seer, mystic, clairvoyant, and psychic diagnostician. He was able to heal many people of their illnesses by going into a trance meditation to determine their disease's roots and discover a cure.

Also famous is the story of Victor Race, who was regarded as a "slow-witted" person. Race was a peasant, yet he could diagnose and cure himself of his disease. But he didn't stop at that. He also helped countless other people with their illnesses by inducing a trance to find solutions to these diseases.

Besides these, there are many other reports of people with psychic abilities around the world. Many of these people come from different cultures. Still, they all had psychic powers. This establishes there are no exceptions to becoming a psychic. Anyone can become a psychic if they are willing to look within themselves.

Suppose you are unfamiliar with the true meaning of psychic. In that case, the first thing that comes to your mind when you hear the word "psychic" may be a person in a dimly lit room with crystal balls, contraptions, fog machines, and other things used to manipulate supernatural events or happenstances. I refer to this as "smoke and mirrors."

You have likely learned that psychics are dubious and fraudulent people from childhood – basically, scammers out to exploit you. So, even if you have experienced an otherworldly occurrence at an early age, you have probably discredited it based on your perception of psychics. Thanks to the media, we neglect psychic occurrences because they aren't as glamorous and dramatic as portrayed in the movies and TV shows we are familiar with.

Most people don't know it, but mediums and psychics are different. I often meet people who think that being a medium and being a psychic is the same thing. A few even use both terms interchangeably. They may seem like the same thing to a person with little to no knowledge of both terms, but there is a distinctive difference.

Unlike psychics, mediums obtain information through channeling or temporary possession. In other words, they are usually possessed by otherworldly beings who pass information through them, but there are psychics with the ability to be mediums.

These are often referred to as psychic mediums. Psychic mediums obtain information through extrasensory perception, but the critical factor is that they can communicate with otherworldly beings. Communication often takes place through their psychic senses. This means that a medium may also be a psychic, but a psychic isn't necessarily a medium. As someone inclined toward psychic practices, it is best to learn the difference between both terms and not misuse them.

There are usually three ways that mediums can help a person. The first is to help you channel recently deceased spirits for communication. Suppose you have a dead relative you would like to communicate with for valuable information. A medium or a psychic medium can help you obtain the information by inducing a trance through which they channel your deceased relative's spirit.

The second way that mediums may use their abilities is to provide medical (physical) relief to a person whose illness seems incurable by science. To do this, a medium would have to channel benevolent spirits willing to help. The spirits will help ascertain the root of the illness and find the cure, which may be as simple as using a crystal.

The third is that mediums can use their powers to solve crimes, especially those that seem unsolvable.

Any psychic with the ability to induce trances and channel spirits may also do the same things as a medium. But this does not mean that psychics and mediums are the same.

As a psychic, you learn of your abilities in two ways. The first is that you naturally become conscious of the fact that you were born with psychic powers. Growing up, you may realize that you usually know things that other people don't know. For instance, you may see things that others claim they can't see. If this is the case with you, it means you are more predisposed to the powers than others. The second way psychic powers materialize is through traumatic or life-threatening experiences. This means if you are not already seeing signs of being psychic, a near-fatal accident, or any other event that causes physical or emotional trauma may trigger your psychic senses.

Psychic development is easily achieved with consistent training and practice. But know that opening up your psychic pathways leaves you vulnerable to the aftereffects and consequences of the psychic practice. This means you must be ready to overcome any fears you may have about becoming a psychic. That way, dealing with the consequences becomes easier for you.

The origin of the word "psychic" is from the Greek word "psyche," which means spirit, soul, mind, etc. By extension, the meaning also refers to thoughts, emotions, and sentiments. Perhaps being a psychic is the same as being a psychologist. The only difference here is that psychics take the mind's study to a higher spiritual level. Instead of just focusing on the mind as psychologists do, psychics extend their study to the soul or spirit. Although your spirit is a divine entity, it dramatically affects your feelings, thoughts, moods, etc.

You can see people's thoughts, feelings, or intentions by reading their auras. Aura reading is also part of psychic development.

To understand who a psychic is, there are few things you must learn by heart. Knowing these things will help you correct any misconceptions you may have about psychics and psychic development. More importantly, they will change your perception and attitude toward extrasensory perception.

One of the vital pieces of information to have about psychics is that they cannot tell you the future in full precision. Yes, this is contrary to what most people believe. You may have heard or read that psychics can accurately predict the future, but this isn't exactly right as a psychic. Training and honing your psychic skills may give you insight into events yet to occur. It does not mean you will predict the event exactly as it is about to happen.

The future is a dynamic thing, so it is impossible to tell it in full precision. An authentic and genuine psychic would never tell you they can see your future precisely as it is. Instead, they help you understand that the future is undefined. You create the future as you make individual decisions and progress in life. What psychic development can do for you is to help you decide to achieve your desired future.

Being a psychic means being extremely sensitive, making you sense energy and other things you cannot see with your psychic pathway locked. A point I should reiterate is that we are all intuitive and sensitive to an extent. Everyone is born with their intuition and psychic senses intact. The difference between a psychic and a non-psychic is that the non-psychic is yet to awaken their psychic senses. If you have never engaged in psychic activities before, it is safe to say that you are a non-psychic. The psychics you know or hear about are not unique or different from you. Suppose you choose to hone and refine your psychic abilities. In that case, that is all you need to identify as an authentic psychic.

Finally, I should note that even though we may all have different abilities, psychics are the same around the world. The difference in abilities stems from the most active psychic sense (s) in everyone. For instance, if your dominant psychic sense is clairsentience, you are most likely to fare well as a psychic medium. On the other hand, an individual with clairvoyance as their primary psychic sense is more likely to perform well as an energy reader. Never forget that everyone has diverse views, experiences, and backgrounds. Naturally, these factors influence how they interpret readings through psychic channels.

The first step to understanding your psychic senses' power is to divorce this misleading perception of psychics. You need to dissociate "psychic" from deception or fraud. Of course, I'm not neglecting the fact that there are charlatans who exaggerate their abilities ridiculously or even ultimately make them up. People like this often rely on tricks to do psychic readings. They are certainly not real psychics. It is much better to describe them as con artists who exploit the gullibility and vulnerability of others. Once you understand this, you become more open to understanding who a genuine psychic is.

An authentic psychic is an individual with the ability to perceive beyond the physical world. Such individuals can use their extrasensory gifts to obtain the information they ordinarily can't acquire with their normal senses. It is difficult to define what to deem as "normal" senses. We have all been conditioned to believe that perception is limited to the physical. Hence, we have a reasonably concrete view of reality.

Due to this conditioning, you might assume that the sky is blue to everyone or that everyone can detect mood changes. But when you expand your knowledge of the sensory spectrum, you will find that not everyone knows the existence of other senses beyond the ones we are all familiar with. This is how you become conscious of your innate psychic abilities.

One fundamental knowledge to have about psychic abilities is that they exist on a spectrum. Sure, it is easy to say that someone is "psychic," but if you were asked *what* their psychic ability *is*, you probably wouldn't have an idea. "Psychic" is a rather broad term for a range of abilities and skills that all concern an inherent ability to obtain sensory data on a profoundly spiritual level. Psychic skills vary in intensity and application, which is why it is best to think of them on a spectrum. Just as psychologists describe traits like narcissism on a spectrum based on the degree of intensity, psychic skills should also be imagined on a spectrum. To bring this imagination alive for you, let's use an example of three friends.

The three friends agreed to walk their dogs together at the park on a Saturday. On D-day, the first friend arrives at the park. She finds a spot to sit and keeps her dog nearby. She barely notices that the park is teeming with people and dogs. After a while, the second friend also arrives with her dog. She approaches her friend and notices that she's absorbed in a game she's playing on her phone. Delicately, she calls out to her friend with a gentle greeting. They exchange pleasantries, and she sits down and adjusts the leash on her dog.

Soon, their third friend arrives, and he is immediately overwhelmed by the teeming population at the park. The different sounds, movements, smells, lights, etc., all come at him at once. He instantly knows the complicated relationship between a couple walking their dog nearby. He quickly moves toward his friends to relay his observations. The first friend says that they weren't even aware there were more people than usual.

From the example above, the first and second friends exhibit a relatively normal range of sensitivity. In contrast, the third friend demonstrates more sensitivity. This means that the third friend likely has more powerful extrasensory abilities. He is likely an empath or a highly sensitive person. Relate this example to your own daily experiences. To what degree do you absorb stimuli every day? Which stimuli resonate with you the most? How do the stimuli impact you physically, emotionally, and spiritually? By answering these questions, you are opening yourself up to understanding your psychic gifts on the spectrum. This is the foundation for tapping into your innate psychic senses.

In the next chapter, I will be focusing more on how you can tap into your inherent psychic powers. Remember that the power is already there, but how do you awaken your psychic senses? There are so many processes involved in self-induces psychic awakening. Let's find out what they are.

# Chapter Two: How to Tap into Your Inherent Psychic Abilities

Over the years, you might have lost access to your inherent psychic abilities. But one never loses their gifts. Regardless of what happens in your life, your psychic senses are lying dormant inside you. To awaken them, you need to look within and find them. Now, the problem is, how do you find and tap into your psychic abilities?

The first step is to identify your dominant psychic sense. Different people have different psychic senses. Although clairvoyance is the most known psychic ability or sense, there are tons of other psychic abilities. Knowing this is crucial to your psychic development journey. Start your psychic awakening process without discovering your prevalent psychic sense. You may find yourself trying and trying without achieving a tangible result.

This is because every psychic sense has specific exercises that are tailored to make awakening easier and faster. For example, if clairvoyance is your dominant ability, visualization-based exercises are the best ways to awakening your clairvoyant sense. But what if you are not clairvoyant? If you keep doing clairvoyance exercises, your journey may take you nowhere, but the first step is to identify your psychic sense. Your psychic sense is directly tied to the psychic ability lying dormant inside you.

Suppose you have ever been to a professional psychic. There, you may wonder how the psychics can gather information during a psychic reading. Well, their key is to tap into their psychic sense (s) to communicate with the spirit world. These psychic senses are called the "claims" of intuition. When you get that gut feeling about something you didn't know before, it is one of your psychic senses at work.

A common misconception about the psychic senses is that one cannot have more than one ability. This is not true. One thing about the Clair senses is that you may be more inclined towards one, but you still have all of these senses. This means that even if clairvoyance is your most vital psychic sense, you can still access any other Clair senses.

Ultimately, there are six Clair senses, but only four are generally found in most people. So, I will only be talking about these four.

The first psychic sense is clairvoyance, which you already know. Although many people use "clairvoyant" synonymously with "psychic," it is one of the four Clair senses available to a psychic. Clairvoyance translates to "clear seeing." Clairvoyant people typically receive psychic messages in the form of images. Simply put, they see images that give them information beyond the physical realm.

As a clairvoyant, psychic messages often appear to be in the form of a scene, playing like a movie. Sometimes, I just receive images. Whether it is images or scenes, the peculiar thing is that the messages are metaphorical. For example, suppose I do a reading on a client who is emotionally overwhelmed. There, I might see them carrying a heavy burden on their back. The messages are not always straightforward, so it is up to you to analyze what appears to you to arrive at the literal meaning.

As a clairvoyant psychic, the images you receive when you do a reading for your clients will always be different depending on each client's situation and other factors, such as their background and physical and emotional states.

To tap into your clairvoyance sense, the most essential thing you can do is to always pay attention to images that pop randomly into your head out of nowhere. Chances are that these images are psychic messages you need to analyze.

Clairaudience is the second Clair sense. It is the psychic ability to hear voices without using your physical ears. If you are clairaudient, psychic messages may come as if someone were speaking out loud in your head. Often, the voice will sound to you like your own, but you can tell it is not your voice. It will never be harsh, cruel, or tormenting. Clairaudient messages come in an even and calm voice.

Usually, clairaudient messages are direct and straightforward. You don't have to analyze anything. Suppose you want to make a big decision, and you use your psychic ability to discover whether to make that decision or not. A clairaudient message may tell you to "wait until the summer is over." Being clairaudient means you will receive short and brief messages.

The message may be a single number or word. When this happens, you naturally need analysis to make sense of the message. If you receive a single word, you may need to tie it back to something in your life to get the actual message or meaning. For example, let's say you are doing a reading for another person, and you hear "15." It can mean different things.

A typical meaning might be that something traumatic happened to the client at 15, causing blocks and obstructing their life's progress. To get the true meaning of the number, you have to work with your subject. Clairaudient messages are sometimes poetic, so you will have fun if your dominant psychic ability is clairaudience.

The most basic way to tap into your clairaudience sense is to pay attention to voices that pop in your head. You also need to become more in tune with your intuition to unlock your clairaudient potentials. Clairaudience is sometimes the dominant psychic ability in mediums and psychic mediums.

The third Clair sense is clairsentience, which means "clear feeling." It is the dominant psychic ability in empaths and highly sensitive people. As a clairsentient, you receive psychic messages in the form of feelings. If you can tell the particular emotion an individual is feeling, you may be a clairsentient psychic. Clairsentience makes you read other people's emotions, receive gut instincts, or get information about the energy moving through your environment.

When I read a client, I always get a feel for their energy. I can tell if they are feeling serious, bubbly, sad, or nurturing. When I get a chill after meeting a client, I know that they have come for something vital. If a client is physically ill and they don't even know it yet, I can tell by getting a feel of their energy. In other cases, I feel the physical symptoms as soon as I come in contact with the client.

If your dominant psychic ability is clairsentience, you can also do all these. That is the point of a clear feeling. It means you can tell the emotion and energy of people you meet exactly as they experience them.

One tactic I used to strengthen my clairsentience ability was to write down in a journal whenever I get a powerful feeling I can't seem to shake. If you do this, you will be surprised at the number of messages you can pick up intuitively. Most people receive clairsentient messages without even realizing it. Keeping a journal of your intuitive feelings is a sure way to tap into your clairsentience ability. The more you recognize the messages, the better you will become at picking upon them.

The fourth and final Clair sense, which you should know about, is claircognizance. This means "clear knowing." It is the psychic ability to know without previous information about a situation, event, person, or object. When a client comes for reading, I know certain things about them before reading them. This is due to my claircognizant ability.

As a claircognizant psychic, you know things without understanding how you even know them. For instance, you can meet a person, and you will be able to tell the exact kind of person they are before you even get introduced. Claircognizance is like receiving a download of information into your brain's hard drive. This happens within seconds, making you feel like the information has been there all along.

To tap into your claircognizance sense, just look within yourself whenever you need answers to anything. Intimately ask your intuition for the solution or answer to any problem you want to solve. If your prevalent psychic ability is claircognizance, you will find the answer somewhere within yourself. Your intuition is there to listen and give you answers whenever you want them.

These are the four Clair senses, which you should be familiar with. Knowing your Clair senses is one step to awakening your psychic abilities. The more important thing is to do things geared toward helping you achieve the psychic awakening you seek.

There are several exercises you can practice while you develop your inherent psychic abilities. These exercises can be combined or practiced individually. It all depends on you and your schedule. The good thing is that you don't have to practice all the techniques every day. Only doing one technique per day can go a long way in helping you access your dormant psychic abilities. It is best to start with whichever of the techniques is the easiest for you to do. The more you practice, the better you will become at all the exercises, even the seemingly difficult ones. In just a few months, you may be amazed at the level of accomplishments you have amassed in your journey.

# Meditation

Meditation is the key to connecting with the deepest levels of your soul. Without meditation, you simply cannot unlock your psychic abilities because there is no other way to connect with that part of you. It allows you to raise your vibration on the same wavelength as the spiritual and otherworldly beings that will bring your psychic messages.

Raising your vibration is a critical part of psychic awakening. Unless you reach a high level of vibrational energy, psychic awakening may be practically impossible for you. Spirit operates at a very high frequency, and you must, as well, if you want to connect.

Daily meditation puts you in a relaxed, calm, and aware state, making it easier to increase your energetic vibration. The more you meditate, the more connected to Spirit, universal energy, and your higher self you become. Fortunately, meditation takes little of your time. All you need is 10 to 15 minutes of daily meditative exercise to keep your vibration on a high frequency.

Naturally, you can meditate anytime you choose, but it always helps you find a good time. The time you choose should be when you feel alert and aware the most. More important, it should be a time when you may practice without distractions and interruptions.

You can meditate early in the morning when you are fresh out of bed and confident you won't fall asleep. You can also choose right before bedtime when you are done with all the hassles of your daily activities. If it works for you, midday is also an excellent time to meditate. The point is to make sure that the time you choose for meditation is right for you.

When you first start meditating, you may think you have to complete 10 to 15 minutes of practice. How long you meditate should depend on the time that is right for you. There is no definite amount of time for meditation. Everything depends on the person involved; in other words, you. Even if you can manage only five minutes every day, that works. You have the liberty to gradually increase the length of your meditation time the more you practice and become better at it.

I like meditation because it is so relaxing and calming that sometimes I forget myself in the process. This helps me spend more time meditating, and it will probably happen to you. The key is to choose a timeframe that does not cause discomfort. Start slowly and build yourself up from there.

A suitable venue is vital in meditation. The place you meditate should be somewhere you are comfortable, but not to the point of sleepiness. It should also be where you are less likely to be distracted, disturbed, or interrupted. Your meditation should be quiet and peaceful, making it easier for you to focus your mind. When you meditate, you can sit in a chair or on the floor. What matters is that you sit comfortably.

Sitting comfortably is essential, but don't be too comfortable. Sit in an upright position, so you don't slouch. This makes it harder to lose focus or fall asleep. The best way to sit when meditating is to keep your spine straight, and your shoulders relaxed. Don't allow yourself to feel stiff.

Once you get the sitting position correctly, the next thing is to breathe. Simply breathe. Let go of any attempt to regulate your breath. Just focus on your breathing. There is no pattern of breathing during meditation. If you pay attention to yourself, you may notice you start breathing quickly, but your breathing will become slow and relaxed as you focus your mind.

The key to meditation is to be mindful of your breathing. You take attention from everything else and focus on your breath. Pay attention as you breathe in and out. Focus on the sensation of your breath as you inhale and exhale.

Naturally, your mind will drift away from your breathing. This is normal, and you don't have to fret when it happens to you during meditation. So many thoughts will pop randomly into your head. Don't try to suppress or shun them. Acknowledge the thoughts as they wander into your mind. Any attempt to stop yourself from thinking will only result in more thinking.

What you can do is to notice every thought, feeling, and sensation that comes up while you are sitting in meditative practice. After that, bring your focus back to your breath. Do this every time you notice your mind wandering.

The most important thing in meditation is the focus. Unless you focus, you cannot induce that state of calm and relaxation you seek. Besides breathing, another way you can focus your mind is by chanting mantras. Many psychics prefer mantra meditation. A popular mantra you can use when meditating is:

"Breathing in, I know I am breathing in.

Breathing out, I know I am breathing out."

This mantra is by Thich Nhat, a famous Buddhist monk and spiritual leader.

Meditation need not be difficult, as long as you follow everything we've just discussed. Finally, make sure you have fun as you practice. Don't be hard on yourself. Don't judge yourself when you get distracted. Just focus and breathe.

## Spirit Guides

Your spirit guides are a part of your Divine spiritual teams. They are souls that have agreed to dedicate themselves toward your spiritual and personal growth. They have existed in several lifetimes, meaning they have more experience than you can imagine. They are there to help you notice and pay attention to things you ordinarily wouldn't. They bring valuable things and people into your life. Most importantly, they help you establish a life of serendipity. They can help you with anything.

Spirit guides are there to help you in your psychic and spiritual development journey. Communicating with them is one way you can tap into your psychic abilities. Spirit guides include spiritual teachers, masters, angels, and other spiritual beings. They can help you with anything you ask them. To meet your spirit guide, you have to channel them through meditation. During meditation, you can ask your spirit guides to reveal themselves to you. Then you can seek knowledge and gather information from them. When they appear, you must not filter your thoughts, feelings, and questions. Go with the flow.

Before you start your meditation, you must set the intention to meet your spirit guide. It's viable your guide won't appear to you on the first try. Don't relent. It just means you need more practice. More important, it means you have to establish trust with your guide.

Visualization will help you in meeting your spirit guide. It is a very effective way of opening up your psychic portals to tap into your abilities. Combining meditation with visualization is a useful technique for psychic development. Using your imagination, visualize what your spirit guides look like.

What do your guides look like? How do they dress? What are their names? What about their personalities?

Answer these questions and write them down in a journal. Whenever you are ready to meet your guides, use your answers to visualize. Your guides will appear to you precisely as you have imagined them to be. Let your imagination flow so you can establish a stronger connection with your spiritual team.

Communicating with your spirit guides requires that you have a sacred space dedicated to establishing that connection. The first time you try to connect with your spirit guide, choose a place where you can comfortably interact with them. You can connect with the guides anywhere you want, but choosing a specific space where you can always hang out comfortably can help you. I recommend your meditation spot because you need to raise your vibrations before they can connect with you.

Spirit guides are invisible, but, like I said, visualizing them can make communication easier for you. It may be hard for you to trust them on your first few tries, mostly due to being a beginner. But know that you can ask them for signs and answers. Asking for signs is a way to build trust between both parties. When you sleep, you become more open to the spirit world. This means that seeing your guides is easier when you are in the dream world. Before you go to bed, try asking your guides to connect with you. Do this with a strong belief they will. Then, you can seek guidance on any issue where you seem lost.

The most important thing is to open your mind and heart to your spirit guides. Look for signs and embrace that there are vast possibilities with your guides.

# Psychometry

Psychometry is the practice of reading an object's energy through touch. It is one of the most effective and fun-filled ways to hone your psychic abilities. You will undoubtedly have a lot of fun practicing psychometry. I always tell beginners to psychic development to make psychometry a vital part of their daily exercises. That feeling of holding a physical object to read its energy boosts confidence and provides a sense of security. It can help you develop all of your psychic senses from clairvoyance to clairsentience. Practicing psychometry is also helpful if you have plans to become a medium.

Using psychometry, you can read the energy of an item to get information about it. You sense the energy, see images, smell things, and hear sounds, which give you insight into the history of the object and its owner. If you are already good at the art of psychometry, you only have to be near an object to read it. But as a beginner, you have to hold the object.

You are likely wondering how psychometry can give you information about an object. It's relatively straightforward. When you touch an object in your home, you leave your physical imprint on the object. But what you may not know is that you also leave your energetic imprint. You are made of energy, like everything else in the universe. You leave your imprint on everything you come in contact with. This means that every object you touch has a vibration of your energy impressed on them. Psychometry allows you to read the energy impressions left on objects. The more the energetic imprints on an object, the more information you can gather from the object.

To practice psychometry:

- First, get rid of any residual energy by washing and drying your hands.
- Get the energy flowing through your hands by rubbing them together for several seconds.
- Next, let your palms face each other with a little distance between them. Pull and draw your palms apart without letting them touch each other. Feel a heavy sensation between the palms. This is the feel of energy flowing. If you don't feel it, rub your hands together for a few more seconds.
- Find a physical object like a ring or bracelet and hold it gently in your hands. You can use any item, but make sure it is worn or used frequently. Use an object that does not belong to you or someone you know. Consider asking a friend for a family heirloom you can use for practice.
- Gently close your eyes and let yourself relax. Do a quick meditation if you have to.
- Pay attention to the sound, smells, and images that come to your mind as you hold the item in your hands. What do you see, smell, hear, and feel?

As you focus, the information will come to you about the owner of the item you are holding. I should note that emotional energy is the strongest you will get from any item you practice psychometry on. The most powerful emotions that emanate are love, fear, and hate.

Note you can use psychometry to practice mediumship and channel the spirit of a departed loved one. To do this, you need the photo of the departed person or an item dear to them while they were alive.

Other ways you can tap into your psychic abilities include:

- Taking a walk in nature
- Visiting antique store to practice energy reading
- Honing your intuition with third eye meditation
- Joining a psychic development group
- Taking courses on psychic development
- Keep a journal to record and track your progress as you practice daily

The bottom line is that you need to practice consistently to unlock your inherent psychic abilities. So, be willing to put the work in!

# Chapter Three: Psychic Tools

Whether you are a beginner or an experienced psychic, you can use lots of tools to enhance your abilities. The point of using psychic tools is to help you consult metaphysical and spiritual beings with a little help. You don't need these tools. But having them can help you master your abilities much faster. Note that not all psychics need tools to get a reading done. Many have mastered the art of using just their intuition and psychic senses for reading. This is especially easy when they have more than one dominant psychic sense.

When you have more than one extrasensory ability, they are bound to overlap during readings. This gives you access to different facets of information during a psychic reading. To do readings without psychic tools, you have to be relaxed and calm. Unless you put yourself in a tranquil state, you may find it hard to connect with your innate information source. Relaxing makes your energy and spiritual field easy to read. As you have learned, the best way to do this is to meditate before you get started. This helps you stay connected to your psychic senses and the spiritual world.

Psychic tools include a range of items you can easily get or create by yourself. To make your learning easier, I have included instructions on how you can make homemade psychic tools without having to spend a lot of money. Suppose you would rather buy the items instead of DIY-making them. There, you can easily find them in online stores where they sell esoteric items. Below are tools that can be combined with your inherent psychic abilities to make you powerful.

## Pendulum

A pendulum is an effective tool for diving deep into the collective consciousness of the universe. Naturally, this also means you can use it to tap into your subconscious and higher consciousness. It does not matter what you are looking for – whether it is a straightforward answer or something a little more in-depth, a pendulum can help you gain more insight into any situation. Throughout history, pendulums have been used effectively for finding lost objects.

People don't believe it, but pendulums can also access spirits. You can use this tool to gain spiritual guidance from the Divine. The good thing about using pendulums for your psychic readings is that they help you get fast and accurate answers to whatever problem. Suppose you want to know about your relationships, career, destiny, or life path. There, a pendulum reading can help you gain knowledge.

To use a pendulum for reading, you have to hold on to the attached chain, allowing it to move and swing freely. A swinging pendulum merely is guiding itself to the answers you seek. As it swings, it is moving through your deepest thoughts, feelings, and energy. The pendulum movements are what you have to interpret to get your answers. Coupled with your extrasensory gift, you should have no trouble with interpretations. If you are claircognizant, the answers may just come to you as you watch the pendulum move and swing.

You can easily buy a pendulum at any physical or online store that sells psychic-related items. If you would rather make your own, below are the instructions to guide you. Note you can make one from wood, plastic, cork, crystal, or even metal. There are different items in your home that can be used to make one quickly. To make your pendulum, you will need a long chain, preferably 15 to 18 inches, to attach the pendulum to. Make sure that the necklace's clasp is still functional. You will also need an adult ring, which could be gold or silver.

- Open the necklace clasp and insert your gold or silver ring through the hole. Close the necklace clasp. Do this so the ring moves freely without falling off.
- Gently place the elbow of your right (or dominant) hand on a flat surface, like a table. Extend your forearm vertically from the table. Then, hold your pendulum so the ring is about 2 inches from your fingers.
- The pendulum will start swinging. As it swings, label the swing motions. Suppose it moves left to right first. You can decide that it a "yes." A right to left motion may be labeled "No." An up and down motion could be "Unknown." This will help you understand what the spirits are saying when you conduct a pendulum reading.
- To test your new pendulum, hold it between your forefinger and thumb. Then, ask a question you know the answer to. For example, you may ask, "Did it rain yesterday?" Check if the pendulum's swing motion answers the predetermined question accurately.
- Repeat the above with at least ten different questions that have predetermined answers. Doing this will help achieve certainty about the movements of the pendulum. Depending on how it goes, you may be required to switch up the previously predetermined labels for the swing motions.

Make sure that the pendulum you make swings as freely as possible. The best way to make sure of this is to see that the holding chain is neither too short nor thick. If it doesn't move as freely and easily as it should, you may need to change the attached chain or ring.

Switch it up until you find one just the right size and gives the desired results.

I recommend that you experiment by making multiple types of pendulums with different materials and chains. Make one with plastic, copper, crystal, or wood. Check whichever works best. Remember that all psychics are different, meaning that what works for you may not work for another person and vice versa.

Before using the pendulum, put yourself in a relaxed and calm state. Otherwise, you may get a lot of answers with which you are not comfortable. Being relaxed reduces your chances of getting negative and conflicting answers.

## Tarot Cards

Tarot cards are one of the most popular tools for psychic readings. Many people are comfortable with them because they are easy to read and understand. You will find many psychics that use them to seek answers to their deepest questions, even on the internet. If you are curious and inquisitive, tarot cards can help you unravel yourself. Learning to read and interpret tarot is a lengthy process. You are bound to start with more questions than answers. It takes time to learn the meaning of the cards. A lot of practice is also required.

When you first get started with tarot, you may find yourself overwhelmed and confused by the sheer amounts of cards. The cards are plenty, and you need to master them all to a reasonable extent. Initially, tarot cards were used for games. They did not become a part of the divination practice until the 18th century. Tarot deals in universal symbols, meaning that the cards and the stories behind their meanings expand beyond culture, time, and continents.

When you buy your pack of tarot cards, you may notice that the cards have distinctive titles. They are also numbered from 0 to 21. On some cards, these are numbered from 1 to 22. Other cards are numbered in the usual way you find on your traditional card deck.

They come with kings, queens, and aces divided into two: the major arcana and the minor arcana. The major arcana comprises all cards without suits. But the minor arcana has cards labeled as wands, cups, swords, and pentacles. A standard tarot deck has 78 cards, 22 in the major arcana and the remaining 56 in the minor arcana.

The cards of the major arcana represent archetypes. They suggest major patterns, themes, and lessons for you or the querent (the subject of your reading) to pay attention to. Different cards stand for the impending change. For instance, if you get the Tower, which is one of the major arcana cards, it means you will experience a huge change to be life-altering.

Note that all the cards of the major arcana are not created equally. Card names may be altered, depending on the deck. Thankfully, the cards always come with extensive information you would do well to read up on before practicing. This will make things easier for you.

The tarot deck's minor arcana comprises cards representing the challenges, triumphs, joys, fears, annoyances, and hopes you experience every day. Remember that just because we call it the minor arcana does not mean that the issues represented are unimportant. "Minor" means they are transient and less far-reaching than issues that appear in the major arcana cards. Also, minor arcana issues are easier to attend to.

The minor arcana is segmented into four suits, as I said. These are the wands, cups, swords, and pentacles. Each is linked to one aspect of the human experience. Swords are connected to cognitive processes and decision-making, wands are related to motivation and action, cups represent emotions and feeling, and pentacles are linked to material things, such as finances and works.

Depending on the kind of deck you buy, they may be mixed up. But these are the general meanings for the suits in any minor arcana.

If you don't want to buy tarot cards, you can, of course, make your deck at home. I suggest that beginning psychics do this because it makes tarot much easier to master. The decks will have a much more specific meaning to your life, meaning that the spirits' answers become more accessible.

Below are the steps involved to make your deck of tarot cards for psychic readings:

- Find a large piece of thick paper where you can cut out 78 pieces of card. The cards can be any size but be sure to put shuffling into consideration when cutting. Note how they feel in your hand and how shuffling will be. I suggest using card stock to guarantee durability.

- As you have learned, a deck of tarot has a single set of 22 cards and another four sets of 14 cards. So, remember this when cutting the 78 cards.

- When you have finished, you will need to design the card and name the minor arcana's suits. The most common design used by beginners is the Rider-Waite-Smith deck. Most resources for learning the meaning of cards follow this design. Know that personal design and deviation can help you achieve more profound meanings.

- Next, you need to sketch the card designs and add labels to them. Consider trying your best imitation of the symbols on the Rider-Waite-Smith deck for your cards.

- Finally, draw or paint the back design on your deck. You can make it simple or complex. It depends on what you like.

That's it. You have your homemade tarot deck to use for psychic readings. You can shuffle and learn the meanings. While drawing and creating your deck, you will have developed a sense of familiarity with each card. You will find this helpful as you master the art of using tarot cards for psychic development.

Unwavering concentration is vital to tarot reading. How you shuffle cards does not matter. What matters is how invested you are in the process. If you are not as invested as you should be, you may end up missing a lot of subtle details.

You shouldn't fret or worry if you didn't learn all the cards' meanings at once. Take your time. One of the critical parts of the whole process is that you end up developing and enhancing your intuition.

# Crystals

Crystals are beneficial gemstones proven to contain spiritual energy. A crystal reading involves mastering these natural resources' many properties and how they can be used for the highest, divine purpose. Just like you, crystals also have energetic and vibrational powers. This means you can use them to increase or enhance your vibrational state. More importantly, you can use them to strengthen your connection to Spirit.

These gemstones' powerful healing properties are functional on both physical and nonphysical planes. Each has an intense and unique concentration of vital energy, thanks to the earth's mix of minerals. As a psychic, you need to know which stones are the most spiritually resonant. Highly resonant stones interact with your energy field so it uplifts and focuses it. Your energy field comprises physical, mental, emotional, and spiritual bodies, which all vibrate at varying frequencies. All these bodies can be positively affected by crystals.

Knowing how to use crystals and gemstones for psychic readings is a fundamental part of esoterism. Crystal reading involves using them to generate and interpret psychic messages. You can also tune into your energy field to discover which stones will significantly benefit your life at a specific moment in life.

The best thing about crystals is that they can also be incorporated into tarot and oracle readings. This greatly increases your chances of getting the answers and solutions you seek. Stones you can use for psychic readings include:

- Sodalite
- Amazonite
- Chrysocolla
- Blue Lace Agate
- Black Tourmaline
- Herkimer Diamond
- Clear Quartz
- Fluorite
- Amethyst
- Azurite

These stones can be used for a range of purposes. Sodalite and Amazonite are great for triggering and maintaining a state of calm during psychic readings. Meditating with these crystals will induce a sense of peace and calm should you receive information you do not particularly like. Clear Quartz is excellent for improving clarification and understanding during reading. It is associated with the crown and third eye chakra, meaning it can help you make sense of your reading and the messages you receive.

Blue Lace Agate and Chrysocolla are effective for ensuring good communication with Spirit when doing a reading. Suppose you are doing the reading for someone else. There, they help you relay received messages articulately to your client or subject. Both stones are tied to the throat chakra. Blue Lace Agate is called the "Stone of Articulation."

You can store your energy crystals and tarot deck together in the same place. Note you don't necessarily need all the stones listed above. They are simply recommendations on the kinds of crystals you should consider getting for psychic practice and development.

The most crucial thing is to go along with your intuition when choosing crystals and stones that can be used in psychic readings.

# Runes

The literal meaning of the word "Rune" is "something secret" or "something hidden." Runes didn't become widely known until the 1980s. Only the most regarded mystics knew and understood the divinatory power of runes. In case you are unfamiliar with runes, they are ancient symbols that serve as esoteric and divinatory tools. Most people assume that runes symbols come from the Latin language, but they are from ancient Germanic languages that predate Latin.

Over the years, they have evolved to express a more symbolic nature. They are now utilized for specialty use. They often come in the form of wooden tiles and beads or glass. Each symbol on each has a specific meaning and message attached. Of course, the messages are from Spirit. To translate the meanings, you must learn the art of rune reading. Psychics who use runes for readings are called runes psychics.

As a rune psychic, you have the knowledge and expertise to consult rune stones for spiritual and divinatory purposes. Even if you don't want to become a master rune psychic, you can learn the basics of rune reading to help your psychic journey. Using runes in psychic readings can help you gain insight into any situation. You may also use runes as an intermediary for clarifying the messages you receive from your spirit guides. You may also use runes as a medium for conversing with the universe to make predictions.

Incorporating runes into your readings can help you establish a strong connection to the Source. This allows you to intuitively interpret psychic messages in tandem with your prevalent psychic ability. To put it simply, the presence of runes during a reading can heighten your dominant psychic sense to where messages become intuitively clear and meaningful to you.

As the querent, you have to start the reading with a specific question or intention. Or you can do a general reading to see if Spirit has anything to tell you. Like in a tarot reading, you have to spread out the rune beads or tiles, after which you do the reading and interpretation.

You may consult Spirit through Runes whenever you need clarity on something. Suppose you have a major or even minor decision to make. In that case, rune reading can help decide which direction to go. A rune spread is a means of getting an explicit picture of what lies ahead of you.

# Astrology

Many people believe that astrology and psychic practices are detached from one another, but this is not true. For hundreds of years, different cultures worldwide have studied the planets and star movements to access divinity. Although astrology is a whole subject in esoterism in its own right, it can be used for a psychic reading. If you study astrology, it will directly affect your psychic growth.

Astrology is all about the alignment and placement of the stars and planets. It is based on the idea that the position of the planets and alignment of the stars during the exact moment of a person's birth influence every facet of their human life, including personality, karma, purpose, and overall mood. If you have any inclination towards the practice of astrology, you have likely observed that you share similarities with people of the same sun sign.

An astrology reading involves combining and incorporating the influences of your Sun sign, Moon, and Ascendant. Suppose you would like to gain insight into why events in your life unfold how they do or the level of compatibility between you and another person. In that case, an astrology reading can help with that. Add astrology to your natural intuitive abilities, and your psychic gifts will be as powerful as you envision.

Astrology isn't something you can fully understand or used just from reading a few sentences. To use astrology as a psychic tool, you need a resource focused on teaching you just that. Natal charts are complicated, so you might need a mentor to make the learning process easier.

These are essentially the best psychic tools you might need in your journey. Having these tools can make practice more manageable for you, but that doesn't make them compulsory. Use them only if you want to. If you would rather be a no-tool psychic, working on your third eye is the best way to go. Doing that will sharpen your intuition and psychic senses to where third-party tools don't matter. It will be just you and your psychic senses.

# Chapter Four: Understand the Astral Body

Have you ever had an OBE? An OBE is an out-of-body experience. It involves your astral body separating from your physical body. It usually occurs when you are in a dream state. Right now, you are probably wondering what an astral body is. To help you understand this concept, I will break it down.

When you look at yourself in the mirror, you can see your physical body. You can see it because it is visible. Contrary to what you may think, the physical body isn't your only body. It is only a small subset of what makes up your whole human system.

You comprise two parts; your physical body you can see and another one you cannot see unless you train yourself to use your third eye. The second part is your energy body. You may also call it your energy field. Remember that I have mentioned the human energy field sometimes in the previous chapter. Well, your energy body is what I have been referring to.

The energy field is widely known as the aura. It is a mix of lights and colors that hand around your physical body. The aura is invisible to the human eye, which means you need to open your third eye if you want to see it. Psychics see the invisible body as a bright energy field that interpenetrates the body and extends about 6 inches from the body. Your energy field is interconnected with your physical body. Whatever affects your energy body will usually reflect in your physical body, and vice versa.

Remember that the energy field cannot exist as a separate entity, meaning it depends on your visible physical body's existence. Just like the body you can see, your energy field has things like a head and body, including arms and legs. The energy field exists because it is vital to the proper functioning of your material body. The body's primary function is to absorb vital energy from the universe and share it around your material form. In doing this, it is energizing your physical form.

The aura or energy body is also a kind of blueprint or mold for the physical body. Without its blueprint, your physical body would have continually changing features due to never-ending metabolism. Essentially, this suggests that the existence of the energy body is crucial to your physical health. As I have likely mentioned, anything that affects the energy field automatically affects the physical body.

Now, your energy field contains different layers and bodies, one of which is the astral body. You may also call it the spiritual body. The astral body is connected to your physical body. It is your one link between the physical plane and the higher (nonphysical) planes. This means that your astral body can function in both the physical world and the metaphysical world.

Suppose you want to travel into the astral plane to interact with higher-dimensional beings and do other things. In that case, you need your astral form to do this. The astral body is the form you use when you are in the dream state. When you dream about yourself doing something while sleeping, that is your astral form in your dream. In lucid dreaming, the astral body is also the one in charge.

The astral form cannot operate while the physical body is active, which is why it takes over when you are asleep, but if you learn how to astral project and astral travel, you can discover how to induce the astral state intentionally.

Your energy field has different energy channels through which it distributes energy to your material form. These channels are known as Nadis. It also has energy centers referred to as chakras. The energy centers and channels are essential for ensuring a clean energy system to flow freely to the physical body.

A clear and free flow of energy is key to the functioning of the physical body. Without it, the body cannot function at its peak. You need a clean energy system to maintain wellbeing and essential body functions. Briefly, let's talk about the energy centers and channels.

The chakras are the energy centers. Seven major chakras pump energy through to your physical form. They vitalize your whole body. You can find the chakras in the body's midline, and they go from down to up. When these energy channels are blocked, it can cause pain or illness in certain parts of your body.

Each of your chakras is associated with one part of the physical body. This makes diagnosis easier for energy healers who help with blockages in the energy field. Understanding how the chakras work and how you can keep open to energy is critical. If the chakras are blocked or nonfunctional, you simply cannot access your psychic portal.

## What are the Seven Chakras?

- **Root Chakra:** This is the first chakra, located at the base of your spine. When the first chakra becomes blocked, it often results in physical symptoms such as sciatica, lower back pain, varicose veins, and several immune-related conditions. The root chakra is in charge of the functioning of your spine, legs, feet, kidney, rectum, and immune system. So, any blockage in this chakra will affect these specific parts of your body.

- **Sacral Chakra**: Located between your navel and lower abdomen, this is the next chakra after the root chakra. When the sacral chakra becomes blocked, it causes physical symptoms such as pelvic pain, sciatica, urinary problems, libido problems, and lower back pain. The second chakra controls your sexual function. It also governs your stomach, liver, kidney, upper intestines, pancreas, spleen, and the area around the middle of your spinal column.

- **Solar Plexus Chakra:** Chakra number three is the solar plexus, which you can probably tell from the name, is located in the solar plexus. This chakra is in charge of your upper abdomen, middle spine, liver, gall bladder, spleen, adrenals, small intestines, rib cage, umbilicus, and stomach. Any blockage in the solar plexus chakra may cause physical conditions such as diabetes, pancreatitis, stomach ulcers, indigestion, cirrhosis, bulimia, and many others.

- **Heart Chakra:** Your fourth chakra is the heart chakra, located at the center of the heart. But the heart chakra doesn't just govern the heart; it also controls other parts of the body such as blood, lung, breasts, arms and hands, diaphragm, and the circulatory system. Blockage in this chakra can cause asthma, pneumonia, upper back problems, and general heart conditions.

- **Throat Chakra:** This is the fifth energy center located at the throat, as made clear by the name. The throat chakra regulates functions in your throat, thyroid, mouth, teeth, esophagus, and hypothalamus. A blocked throat chakra may show physical symptoms such as throat ulcer, scoliosis, thyroid dysfunctions, and speech or voice problems.

- **Third Eye Chakra:** Chakra number six is the third eye chakra, possibly the most popular chakra. Even people who aren't invested in esoterism know about the third eye chakra. The third eye is popular across different cultures globally, but all agree that it is the seat of intuition. The third eye controls your brain, pituitary gland, neurological functions, and pineal gland. When blocked, the third eye chakra results in symptoms such as brain tumors, seizures, strokes, spinal dysfunction, blindness, and learning disabilities.
- **Crown Chakra:** This is the final and highest chakra. The crown chakra can be found atop your head, on the crown. It governs the midline above your ears and the top of your head. The crown chakra is the link to forming a connection with the Higher Consciousness, and when blocked, it will cause physical conditions relating to the skeletal system, muscular system, skin diseases, and chronic exhaustion.

The Nadis are the energy channels. They are much more plentiful than the chakras. As the energy channels, the nadis or meridians transport energy through the chakras. They affect your physical health just as much as the chakras. Any disturbance in the transportation of energy from the nadis to the chakras will cause physical disease and illness.

There are 12 major nadis and thousands of other minor ones across different locations in the body. The major nadis are named after their functions. You have the lung, spleen, stomach, large intestine, small intestine, heart, kidney, liver, bladder, heart constrictor, triple heater, and gall bladder nadis. These cover your whole physical system, helping your body maintain a balance. Blockage in the nadis upset the body's balance.

Right now, you are probably wondering what all of these have to do with the astral body and psychic development. Well, energy blockage is generally not good for psychic business. If you suffer from an energy blockage, it will affect your ability to access your psychic portals. It will also obstruct your ability to channel your astral body. Note that astral traveling is a crucial part of psychic practices.

I am saying that your energy system has to be clear and balanced if you want to use your powers. The third eye, as I said, is the seat of intuition. This means you can't access your intuition when the third eye chakra is blocked. Your energy body has to be free of blockages at all times.

The first step to ensuring your system stays free of blockages is to understand what causes energy blockages in the first place.

Your physical body is quite fragile, affected by both internal and external triggers. These often result in energy stagnation or concentration. Most of the time, the triggers result from mental and emotional imbalance. But they can also be caused by poor environmental conditions, unhealthy nutrition, and illness.

When any trigger sets off in the physical body, your energy flow starts diluting. This leads to pain and organ damage. Although blockage directly affects the specific area where it happens, it ultimately has a ripple effect. This means it disrupts the flow of energy to other parts of the body. Naturally, it causes a downward spiral in your energy system's overall functioning and the quality of your health. When this happens, energy healing is the key to getting rid of the blockage and providing relief across your energy system.

The best energy healing techniques used by expert energy healers include Reiki, Ayurveda, Acupuncture, etc. Besides Reiki, you can't do some of these techniques on your own. Below are simple energy clearing and cleansing techniques you can do in the comfort of your own home to make things easier on you.

I should note that your energy field has to be clear at all times to read other people's energy. As you can see, learning these techniques is important.

# Technique 1: Run Energy Through the Chakras

This here is one of my personal favorites for clearing energy. It is an exercise targeted at attuning your mind, body, and emotions with your soul. Doing this restores the balance within your energy system. Getting rid of dense energy improves your connection with the source of energy. This, in turn, enhances your clarity and intuition, allowing you to use your inner guidance to make important decisions and answer vital questions.

Running energy through the chakras is something I recommend you integrate into your daily spiritual activities. Daily practice is how you can get the full benefits of this technique. You can start small - five to ten minutes of your time every day will make a tremendous difference for your whole system.

The process is straightforward. You ground, run, and then clear the energy in your system every morning and evening. As you practice more, your vitality, clarity, and sense of focus increase. Then, you can increase the time you use for your daily dose. I like this technique because you don't need a quiet or tranquil location to do it. You can run energy wherever you are when you feel the need for it. You can even do it when having a heated conversation with another person.

At first, you may not be able to feel anything. This is quite normal. You just need to keep going until you can. Ask the energy to fill you up, and trust it will. As the saying goes, practice makes progress. The more you do it, the better you will become at it, and the more you will gain the benefits.

How do you go about this technique?

**Get Grounded**

First, you have to get grounded. We are rarely ever-present at the moment. Stressors and distractions from the activities of our daily lives abound. They often keep our minds fixated on the past or the future. Getting grounded is a way of immersing yourself in the present moment rather than the past or the future. Mindfulness and presence at the moment is the first step to attuning your mind, body, and emotions with your spirit.

### Step 1: Create a Grounding Cord from Your First Chakra

Sit in an upright position with your arms and legs uncrossed. Place your feet firmly flat on the ground. Imagine at the base of your spine, traveling to the center of the earth, a beam of light originating from your root chakra.

### Step 2: Open Up Your Crown Chakra

Visualize another cord of light traveling from your crown chakra directly up into the heavens to connect with the cosmic energy.

### Step 3: Call Out Your Spirit Home

Call out your full name loudly. Repeat it three times. Your full name is unique to you. By repeating your full name, you call your consciousness into the present moment.

### Step 4: Create Grounding Cords from Your Feet

Awaken the chakras on the base of your feet. With your feet firmly on the floor, envision beams of light traveling your feet to the core of the earth.

### Step 5: Run Energy from the Earth

Once you have successfully created cords running from your feet and first chakra, and a cosmic cord from your crown chakra, it is time to run earth energy up. Call the energy from the earth's core and visualize it traveling into your feet, upwards through your legs, as far up as the crown of your head. Visualize the energy filling up the outer layers of your energy field. Let your aura and body be filled up with this energy. Once filled up, let the energy flush down the cord attached to your first chakra into the core of the earth.

Now, you have successfully grounded yourself through earth energy. The next step is to run your energy.

### Run Your Energy

After successful grounding, you can channel energy through your chakras, clearing blockages and cleaning them one by one. Better than anyone, you know exactly what you want. Allow the healing energy to wash through your body, mind, emotions, and spirit. By doing this, you will have the vitality needed to project the high-vibrational energy that attracts higher-dimensional beings towards you.

### Step 6: Run Divine energy

In contrast to grounding energy, which travels from the earth's core up to wash down the cosmic grounding cord, the divine energy travels downward from the crown chakra through the rest of the chakras until it reaches the center of the earth. Run the energy at least four times and visualize the colors of energy pumping through your body as you run it. There are four colors, and they all represent four types of energy you have to run.

The first is a royal deep-blue color for deprogramming energy. This is targeted towards washing out dense energies from your system. The second is a neon-electric-blue color for clarity energy. It is targeted toward improving clarity and enhancing knowingness. Third, you have a green color for healing energy. You run this energy to heal wounds in the physical and nonphysical systems. Finally, the fourth is a golden color for love and truth energy. Run this to revitalize yourself with light and love. It will remind you of who you are and the extent of your psychic capabilities.

### Step 7: Switch the Grounding Cord

This is the final and most crucial step in this energy-healing technique. Before you round up, you have to replace your grounding cord with a new one. This will help realign and anchor you into the present moment. Allow all residual energies to run down and be released through the old cord. Then, get rid of the cord by visualizing a rose grounded to the earth through the stems. In this context, the rose is a symbol of forgiveness and a way of transmuting toxic energy into light.

Visualize your old grounding cord in the center of the rose and let it explode over a vast body of water, immersing the rose to be rinsed and restored to new.

Anytime you feel like there is a blockage in your energy system, use this technique to clear it out and revitalize yourself.

## Technique 2: Visualize to Release Negative Energy

Visualization is a simple practice that can be done anywhere and anytime. You can do it at work or even while you are in a crowded space. It is normal not to get visualization on your first try. Even if you feel like it is not something you are good at, keep trying. Like the first technique, this also gets better the more you practice.

And this technique is not just about imagination. It involves creating an actual energy shift you can feel in real-time. The process is shown below.

### Step 1: Set an Intention

The first thing you must do is set an intention to release all negative and toxic energy from your system and whatever you may have picked up from other people's aura. You can set your intention by saying, "I release all energy that no longer serves me from my system, whether it is from myself or others. I do this to achieve my highest purpose." Or you can form your intention. Just make sure that it goes along with the theme of what you are about to do – releasing toxic and residual energy and energy blockages.

### Step 2: Establish a Body of Light

Envision a brilliant ball of golden light in the core of your chest. Imagine the light expanding and getting bigger as you exhale. Then, imagine the light expanding as you breathe in and out of your chest. It should get bigger with each exhalation.

### Step 3: Spread the Light

Imagine the ball of light spreading from one part of your body to the next until it is across your entire body. Visualize it in your head, arms, torso, toes, and other parts of your body.

### Step 4: Expand the Light

Envision the light to expand until it is beyond your skin. Let it expand until it is just about an arm's length outwards in all directions.

### Step 5: Wrap Up with Shielding

Shielding is a way of forming a protective shell around yourself to avoid soaking up toxic energy from your environment. It dramatically reduces your chances of suffering energy blockage. It's relatively easy. Just imagine a big bubble of light around you. Picture the bubble as a solid filter covering your whole body completely. Ask the bubble to act as your shield from negative energy while allowing positive energy and love to filter inside. Visualize the bubble filling up with golden light.

That is all. As you can see, this technique is short and straightforward. But more important, it is highly effective for energy cleansing and healing. Incorporating this into your daily activities will make you much calmer, more peaceful, and more balanced. It will also make you less reactive.

Another thing you can do is to use minerals to eliminate all toxicity from your energy body. Get a cup of sea salt and another cup of baking soda. Dissolve both in a warm tub and soak yourself inside to banish toxicity and negativity. To avoid taking a full bath, give yourself a simple foot soak. But don't use a whole cup for a foot soak. Reduce it to a quarter of a cup. This is also helpful with grounding.

In the next chapter, we will be looking at how you can consciously use your astral body to project and travel the astral plane without needing to be in the dream state.

# Chapter Five: Astral Travel

Whether you want to call it the astral body, energy body, or dream body, the fact is that you have a nonphysical body that can be used to travel the nonphysical realms. Everyone has an astral body. The experience of astral projection or traveling is universal. Different people across different cultures have talked about having an out-of-body experience. There is a widely known story about twins who used astral traveling to see each other after separation at birth.

The subtle body of the energy field is the one that projects into a spirit during lucid or unconscious dreaming. Astral traveling and dreaming are intertwined, and they are both regarded as out-of-body experiences. When cultivated, your astral body can exist separately from the physical body, acting as a matrix for your consciousness. Astral projection is one of the spiritual training mediums for cultivating your subtle energy body.

An out-of-body experience is typically involuntary in many people. You may have even had an OBE without realizing it. There have been reports of near-death experiences where people suddenly found themselves floating or hovering in a nonphysical form near their hospital rooms. At the same time, their medical doctors worked on saving their lives. OBEs are typically triggered by trauma, illness and water, food, and sleep deprivation.

Unlike science-recognized OBEs, astral projection is an intentional esoteric practice. By this, I mean it is something you do with the awareness of your consciousness. So, you can simply call astral projection an intentional out-of-body experience. When you astral project, your astral body transcends your physical body. You are basically in a dreamlike state while being fully conscious of your actions and decisions. This is achievable through self-hypnosis and meditation. In your astral state, you can travel through time, space, and dimensions. This might sound like something out of a superhero movie. It happens with people working on connecting deeper with the Divine. Worldwide, astral projection is recognized as a way of deepening your spiritual practices.

Astral traveling is one way you can explore different realms across the universe to strengthen your connection with the source of cosmic energy. The more you travel the astral plane, the more you will probably meet higher-dimensional beings to help you achieve your spiritual and personal goals. Note that the astral dimension is home to many otherworldly beings that could be high-vibrational or low-vibrational.

Learning astral projection and travel is not always as easy as you see in the movies. There is no definitive guide to astral travel. There is no one-size-fits-all guide that everyone can use to learn astral travel. What works for one person may not work for you. Even when it works, it may not work as quickly as it did for the other person. Everyone is unique, and so are their experiences with astral travel.

This does not negate that there are basics that anyone can use to travel the astral plane in their astral body. Before you get the spiritual passport and begin your journey, you have to master these basics. As you should know already, consistent practice is the key to mastering anything in esoterism.

Being a beginner, first master the art of meditating without snoozing or falling to sleep. Before you even project your astral body, start the daily practice of meditating for at least 5 minutes. By doing this, you will learn to calm and focus your mind. Projecting for the first time can be alarming for most people. But being in a state of calm and focus makes it less alarming for everybody. If you can't seem to find your Zen on your own, use crystals discussed in an earlier chapter to meditate.

After mastering the art of entering a calm state with meditation, you might want to learn self-hypnosis. The purpose of this is to help you learn how to enter an even deeper trance-like state. The more it feels like you are in a trance, the better your chances of projecting your astral body and possibly exploring the nonphysical dimensions. Self-hypnosis is similar to meditation, but it makes the astral plane more accessible so you can connect with others. The main difference between meditation and self-hypnosis for astral projection is that self-hypnosis requires you to set an intention and a specific goal. For instance, your intention for channeling your astral body might be to talk to your spirit guide on the astral plane.

Lucid dreaming is another technique you can use for astral projection. Since it is a way of tuning in with your consciousness in a controlled and intentional way, it helps astral traveling. Once you have learned how to put yourself in the trance-like state required for projection, the next thing to do is to tune in with your astral body and transcend beyond the physical.

Before attempting to travel, it helps to master projection first. During meditation or self-hypnosis, try to see your spirit emerging out of the material form. Once you master this, progress to turning around and looking at your physical body. Remember that this is not something that will happen overnight. To be successful, you have to keep practicing. It might take you many meditative sessions before you can even lift your astral form from your material form. Do not let this discourage you.

Once you feel comfortable being in your astral body, you can access and explore the astral realm. You can begin your astral travels if you don't want to travel on the astral plane, no problem. Your astral form allows you to do much more than that. In your astral form, you can explore the limitless space beyond the material world.

If you are wondering what you stand to gain from learning astral projection, there are many benefits. First, your astral form can be used to travel to the Akashic Records location. This is where you can find all the information about your past lives and selves. You may also find information about your future. The Akashic Records is home to infinite knowledge. By accessing the records, you can use whatever information you retrieve to improve your life and accelerate your personal development.

Another benefit of astral projection is that it helps with physical and spiritual healing. Remember I said that the energy body is the blueprint of your material form. I also said that whatever happens in the physical body starts in the energy field first. When you are in your astral form, you have direct access to your aura or energy field. In this form, you can examine your auric field for any blockages or building illnesses. If a disease forms in one of your auric layers, you can tell from examination in your spirit form. You cannot only examine and discover any developing illness or disease, but you can also treat and heal your auric layers before the disease manifests in your material body.

That is not all. Suppose an illness or disease manifests in your physical body before you even realize it. There, you can enter your astral form to heal it with energy. Astral projection can help you explore your past lives, accelerate your personal and spiritual development journey, and heal yourself of disease and illnesses.

Perhaps, the most important benefit of astral projection is that it allows you to connect and communicate with your spirit guides in astral forms. This means you can see and speak with your guides. That is a rare opportunity for you to seek guidance and direction on anything bothering you.

On the astral plane, you don't just find spirit guides. You can also find the spirits of your deceased loved ones. So, if you have loved ones you would like to meet and possibly ask questions, visiting the astral plane is a way to do that. I could go on and on about the benefits of astral projection, but I am sure you understand the drift now.

Now that you know what astral projection and traveling are and what they involve, how do you practice both to reap the benefits we have just discussed?

There are many techniques you can learn to start astral projection. We have as many as dozens. But know that not all of these works as effectively as they should. Yet, two approaches are peculiar to all of these techniques.

The first is to seduce your body into sleep while your mind is wide awake. This approach is tricky because your mind always wants to do what your body is doing. This approach aims to gradually seduce your body into deeper and deeper relaxation levels without the mind slipping into unconsciousness. The second approach involves allowing your body to enter the sleep state and then rolling your dream body out of your material form.

Ancient yogis used to tie two frogs together right before entering the sleep state. The tied frogs would relentlessly cloak as the yogi sleeps. The yogis used the sound to help their awareness/mind stay alert even as the body drifts into sleep. Eventually, they would enter a lucid dream state, or the astral form leaves the body.

Most of the astral projection techniques follow these approaches. Below, I will be explaining the most effective exercises for astral projection and how you can use them.

## The Monroe Institute Technique

This technique was developed by Bob Monroe, a leading researcher in the field of human consciousness. It is recorded in his body of work, "Journeys Out of the Body." Monroe provides a detailed and step-by-step outline of how one can astral project. The technique is one that Monroe personally used for astral travels. In just seven steps, you can use this to project yourself astrally.

### Step 1: Meditation State

Do a quick meditation exercise to induce a relaxed state physically and mentally. Relaxing your body and mind is the foundation of astral projection. You may also do a quick breathing exercise to put yourself in a relaxed state.

### Step 2: Hypnagogic State

Put yourself in a hypnagogic state. In other words, allow yourself to enter a half-sleep state where you are neither asleep nor awake. You can do this by holding a forearm up while the upper arm rests on the ground or bed. As sleep is induced, your arm will fall, awakening you again and again. With consistent practice, you will eventually learn to enter the hypnagogic state without using your arm.

Another way you can enter this state is by choosing an object on which to focus. When other images start entering your head besides the one you are focused on, you have successfully induced the half-sleep state. Passively observe the images to help you maintain the near-sleep state.

### Step 3: Near Sleep

Deepen the near-sleep state. Do this by clearing your mind and watching your field of vision via closed eyes. Don't do anything else for a while. Then, look through the blackness in front of your closed eyelids. You should start noticing light patterns. These have nothing to do with the process because they are merely neural discharges from your eyes. So, ignore them until they disappear from your vision.

When this happens, it means you have entered a deeper state of relaxation. From that point, you will enter a state where you have no awareness of physical sensations in your body. You may feel like you are in a void where your thoughts are the only source of stimulation. The point of this step is to prioritize mental sensations over physical sensations. If you can still feel physical stimulation, it means you haven't entered the desired state yet.

### Step 4: State of Vibration

Induce a state of vibration where you become alert to vibrations around you. When you are in a state of deep alertness, vibrations become more heightened. This is considered the most critical step in this technique, and it can make or mar your attempt at astral projection. Vibrations may feel like mild tingling around your body. They also are more intense, making you feel like jolts of electricity are being shot through your body. In essence, this is your astral body trying to unroll from the material one.

Before you enter the vibrational state, make sure you don't have any jewelry on. Take off any item that has direct contact with your skin. Make sure that the room is dark to where you can't see the light through your eyelids. But don't shut out every source of light. Lie on the floor with your head pointed toward the north. Get rid of all clothing but leave yourself covered, so you feel warmer than usual. The warmth should feel a little uncomfortable for you. Make sure you are in a room where no one will disturb or interrupt you. If possible, lock the door from intruders.

### Step 5: Regulate the Vibrational State

Control your vibrational state by mentally pushing the vibrations into your head. From there, allow them to travel down to your toes. Feel the surge as they pass through your whole body, and you produce vibrational waves from top to bottom. You should produce a wave effect.

To do this, focus on the vibrations in your body. Envision a wave of vibrations coming out of your head and direct it down the rest of your body. Repeat this step until you have mastered the art of producing the waves on command. Once you master this, it means you have reached the point where you can exit your body.

### Step 6: Partial Separation

At this stage, what you need is thought control. You must focus your mind on the idea that you are exiting your body. Do not allow your mind to stray to anything else. Wandering thoughts might end with losing control of your current state. When you are in the vibrational state, you can begin partial separation by first attempting to release one part of your astral form. This could be one of your feet or hands.

You may lift a limb until you feel it touch a familiar surface or object. Then, you may push your limb through the surface or object. After this, return the limb into the physical form. If you do this successfully, reduce the vibrations across your body until you are no longer in that state. End the session and lie down quietly until you are sure you are back to your usual self.

Doing a partial separation first prepares you for the full separation.

### Step 7: A Full Separation from the Physical Body

Detach completely from your material form. You can do this in two ways. One way is to ease out of the physical body gently. Doing this requires you to mentally visualize yourself getting lighter and lighter once you have entered the vibrational state. Imagine how you would feel were you floating upward. Let this thought remain in your mind as you remain in a vibrational state. Allow no other extraneous thoughts to chase it away from your mind. At that moment, you will naturally have an out-of-body experience.

The second way is to roll out of your body. This is called the rotation or rollout technique. When you are in the vibrational state, mentally visualize yourself rolling out of your material body in the same way you turn over in bed. Be sure not to do this physically—virtually rollover out of your physical form into the astral form. You will find yourself next to the physical body, which is now lying motionless. Visualize yourself floating upward, and you should feel as you begin to float.

Congratulations, you have successfully experienced astral projection. Now that you are in your astral form, you can do whatever you want. Explore the astral plane or go see your favorite celebrity in your astral form. There are no limits to where you can explore in your astral state.

# Lucid Dreams

As I mentioned, inducing a lucid dreaming state is another way to enter your astral form and travel the astral plane. Lucid dreaming itself has many techniques that can be used for this purpose. Some are engineered to train you to awaken while having a lucid dream. Others help the mind lucid while the body enters the sleep state.

The moment you enter the dream state, you attain lucidity. You can train yourself to lucid dream with repetition. One method of doing this is to ask yourself multiple times a day for weeks, "Am I in a dream?" or "Is this a dream?" This question becomes repetitive, causing it to become stuck in the part of your mind where you store songs and jingles. It becomes a habit that starts repeating itself. Eventually, the mind will ask you this during an actual dream. If you answer, "Yes, this is a dream," you will automatically attain lucidity.

REM (rapid eye movement) sleep is your best chance to become lucid while already in a dream state. The REM stage occurs in the first two hours after you fall asleep. It also happens in the last two hours before you wake up. Waking up and returning to sleep during the night is one way you can increase your REM sleep timeframe. Using this sleep/wake technique, you can set the alarm to help you wake at intervals during nighttime. Then, you return to sleep, intending to keep your mind awake. If you wake up during a dream, go back to sleep instantly – try to go back to the dream with a lucid mind.

Once you become confident in your ability to astral project, you can start moving through the astral plane. With each successful attempt, the astral state becomes more accessible for you.

Whenever you visit the astral plane, you will meet different energy beings. Not all of these beings are good. Some may be there to suck energy from you. To avoid them, it is best to set an intention before you enter the astral plane. Have a specific goal in mind. For example, you can set an intention to see a loved one that passed on recently. Other intentions you can set include seeing your spirit guides, visiting a memory from the past, seeing into the future, or finding answers to questions about your spiritual development. Intention can be set before or after your astral project. Once you have connected with your astral self, you can consciously send yourself to a specific place on the astral dimension.

After every successful projection and travel, use the previous chapter's energy cleansing techniques to get rid of any unwanted energy you might have picked up while on the astral plane.

As someone new to astral traveling, you may find you can't enter the astral realm as easily as described. This is normal. You may also not reach your set destination on the first few tries. But don't fret – the more practice you put in, the stronger your astral traveling skills will become.

Apart from astral traveling, what is another psychic ability you can work on developing? Find out in the next chapter.

# Chapter Six: Begin Your Mediumship

Mediumship is the psychic practice that involves bringing information from the spirit world to the physical world. A medium is anybody with the ability to do this. This psychic ability is called mediumship because the psychic or medium essentially acts as a middleman, a vessel through which spirits can get messages across to people here on earth. Although you may have seen in the movies that mediums are people who use powerful magic, this is not right.

Everyone, including you, is born with the ability to be a medium. As long as you have a soul with psychic senses, you have the inherent gift. What matters is whether you let it keep lying dormant or you work on honing the ability so it can benefit you and the people around you. Any psychic ability can be made stronger with practice.

Think of your psychic abilities as your body's muscles. When you go to the gym to work on your muscles, the biceps will bulge and come out. This makes you stronger. This is the same with the psychic sense associated with your psychic abilities. You may not realize it, but they are inside you. If you work on them, they too will start to show.

From an early age, you might have had one or more experiences with spirits. I remember seeing my first spirit when I was still at the tender age of 6. Sometimes, your ability to see, hear, and interact with spirit may manifest itself. At other times, a traumatic experience such as losing a loved one might be the key to opening the pathway to that ability. This usually happens because the passed loved one has an important message to get across to you or someone else they knew during their life. If your primary psychic sense is clairsentience, mediumship comes more easily.

If you feel like you are getting signs from someone on the other side, acknowledge and let them know that you are receiving their signs. Acknowledging them means you are more likely to receive more signs. Then, you can keep conversing with them. Sometimes, the spirits may visit instead of sending signs.

Beginning your mediumship is one of the most remarkable things you can experience as a psychic. The first time you connect with the spirit world will feel surreal and magical. You will find yourself filled with a feeling of peace and calm you have possibly never felt before. This goes beyond inner peace. It reflects physically as a sensation of pure love, peace, and acceptance.

Based on movies we watched while growing up, we have been conditioned to believe that ghosts (spirits) are generally malevolent spirits looking to hurt us. In reality, they are the spirits of people we knew while alive, so how could they possibly want to hurt us? You have absolutely no reason to fear spirits. They cannot physically do anything to you. The only thing they can do is inspire weird vibes and feelings in you. Other than that, they are harmless, which is a good thing.

How are you able to communicate with spirits?

Spirits are beings that haven't been able to move on to the other side after their death. Therefore, they are still operating in the same element as you, the Earth element. Due to this, you can communicate with them. Even after death, our spirits or souls live on. The body may die, but the soul doesn't, which is why many people have past lives. When some people die, their spirits remain tethered to the earth due to something meaningful. This leaves them stuck on the astral plane, where they can easily come down to earth. Some require mediums to deal with whatever is keeping them in the earth element.

If you wonder why you would ever need to communicate with spirits, know there are various reasons. One of the basic things you must understand as a medium is that the spirit world is full of guides that can benefit you immensely if you pay attention to their signs. Ghosts are not the only spirits. Mediumship goes beyond communicating with ghosts. Being a medium means you can communicate with just about any spirit, including the highest vibrational ones. You can learn a lot from your connection to spirits and the spirit world. That special connection can assist you in different stages of your life.

The good thing about mediumship is that you can learn it all on your own. However, there are a few things I always advise people just beginning their mediumship.

First, don't start your mediumship by using tools such as a pendulum or Ouija board. If you don't train yourself to connect without tools first, your abilities may depend on the tools. Setting that precedence is dangerous for your development in practice. But what makes it dangerous is these tools are used to open up a portal to spirits. This means that any spirit, not just the one you want to communicate with, can come through that portal.

Yes, the spirits cannot physically harm or hurt you. The problem is that you will have a lot of ghosts hanging around you with stuck energy.

Second, be careful not to lose your focus. Staying focused is an essential tool for any psychic medium. You have to be specific and focused when channeling any spirit. The process requires a lot of concentration because opening up a portal to the spirit world drains you of energy. It is a whole lot of work. If you don't focus on the spirit you want to connect with, you may end up channeling another spirit that will be of no help to you. After using a lot of energy, you may find it hard to refocus and invoke the spirit you want.

Third, listen to your guts. Listening to intuition rarely fails mediums. Sometimes, the spirits communicate with you through your guts. If your spirit guide wants you to know something urgent, you may feel a strong sensation in your gut. It's like when you meet a new person, and you feel a strong compulsion to exchange your contact details with them even though you usually wouldn't do that. That is your spirit guide prompting you through your gut feelings.

To hear what your guts have to say, you, of course, need to quiet your mind. Therefore, my fourth piece of advice is that you quiet your mind at all times. You can't hear spirits when there is a lot of noise and chatter in your mind. There are different ways you can quiet your mind. Discover whichever works best for you. Some things you can do this effect include walking in nature, practicing deep breathing, turning your phone off, and of course, meditating. Once you achieve a quiet mind, your spirit guides can meet you to offer help and guidance.

Pay attention to your dreams because sometimes, spirits send messages through the dream portal. Communication via dreams is a real thing. It is especially a thing with spirits who are still in the early stage of their passing. If they have successfully crossed over to the other side, the only way they can contact you is through dreams. Most of the time, they appear in your dream to let you know they are in a good place. Or they may appear to warn you of something that is yet to happen.

Finally, make writing a vital part of your mediumship journey. Some writing meditations can help you communicate with spirits. It is easy.

- Light a white candle. Sit comfortably. Close your eyes and breathe in deeply. Then, breathe out. Do this for some seconds.

- Say out loud that you would like to connect to the higher vibrational beings available to you as guides.
- Next, as a question, breathe in and out deeply and allow your hands to relax loosely. Then, write down whatever the spirits say to you. They often talk fast, so don't be alarmed if you are writing just as fast.

Follow all these tips, and you will have no trouble connecting with the spirit world. Still, it is possible to have trouble establishing a connection. Don't stress about it. Remember that the whole thing is a process, and you won't necessarily make progress on the first few tries. Just because you want to connect with them instantly does not mean you will. You might take years to perfect this practice.

## How to Tune Into the Spirit World

Tuning in with the spirit world is relatively easy. It all depends on how long you have been engaging in psychic activities. Suppose you have been engaging your psychic senses and sharpening your intuition. In that case, it won't be as hard as it would be for someone new to the whole thing.

Establishing a connection with the spirit world is akin to tuning in to a specific radiofrequency. When you tune in to the spirit, you are raising your vibrational energy. But Spirits lower their vibrational frequency so you can connect with them. Both of you then meet in the middle.

There are three important rules you must never forget whenever you want to tune into the spirit world.

1. Your journey to the spirit world is unique to you. You must respect and honor this.

2. Always say what you encounter. You have no reason to hide from whatever you see when you connect to the spirit world. If you do hide, you will likely lose valuable information that could give meaning to your journey.

3. Trust whatever comes to you first as you open up the portal to the spirit world. The first thing you see is likely to be the most accurate information.

Below are five steps to tune into the spirit world.

• **Set an Intention:** You need to say out loud that you would like to open up the spirit portal to communicate and receive messages from a specific spirit in the spirit world. Clarify whether you are connecting for a personal purpose or on behalf of another person. The Universe hears as you state your intention out loud, and so do the spirits in the spirit world.

• **Meditate:** A simple meditation or breathing exercise to quieten your mind is a necessary step. Using your daily meditation technique, get your logical brain to quieten down. This is crucial for a swift and clear connection with spirits.

• **Listen:** Listen attentively for any sign, symbol, or message from the spirit world. The message may come in the form of songs, images, noise, or anything else. Sometimes, you may not even receive the message immediately. So, you have to pay attention to the events that happen throughout your day. Any coincidence that happens may not be a coincidence.

• **Draw Up a Reading Screen:** If you are a clairvoyant, a reading screen is necessary to receive the spirit's message. The screen is where you will find whatever information spirit has for you in the form of images, pictures, and symbols. Helped by your third eye, visualize a giant movie screen in front of you. Attach a grounding cord to the screen and root it to the core of the earth. Now, ask a question or ask to receive a message from spirit. Be careful not to use a demanding tone. Don't be impatient – let the answer come to you.

As you practice, you will find it easier to connect with the spirit portal. To further help you create a strong connection, here are some tips.

- Don't smudge with sage right before you connect with a spirit. Sage is an ancient herb often used to ward away ghosts and spirits. Using it before channeling a spirit confuses the spirit because they read that as you tell them to leave your space.

- Set up multiple conductors. Spirits sometimes need conduits to deliver their messages properly. Before you attempt to contact a spirit, set up different conductors that can be used for communication. Light a candle, put some water in a glass, and use incense to add scent to the room. You may also install audio and video recording devices in the room. They are effective conductors that can help with transmission from the spirit world to the human world.

Connecting with the spirit world is an opportunity for you to explore the differences between the physical plane and the realm of the dead. Use that opportunity wisely. As you advance your mediumship journey, you can finally introduce the Ouija board and pendulums into your practice as a psychic medium.

# Chapter Seven: Unlock Telepathy

Suppose someone was to ask you to say the first thing that comes to mind when the word "communication" is mentioned. In that case, you'd mention things such as speaking, writing, and even chatting before you mention telepathy. Yet, telepathy is one of the best ways of communicating.

Telepathy simply means communication through the mind. Your mind is much more powerful than you even realize. Yes, science says that the mind is a powerful entity. Still, even science has yet to unravel the extent of the power of the mind. Most of us don't even understand how awesome this is.

F. W. H. Myers coined the term "telepathy" in 1882. Myers was a British researcher interested in psychical practices. When he coined this term, he was researching the possibility of "thought transference." Simply put, thought transference was firstly defined as a phenomenon in which two people's thoughts coincide, requiring a causal explanation. Later, it was defined as "a transmission of thought independently of the recognized channels of sense."

From this definition, you can tell everything that telepathy entails. Telepathy is a psychic ability that allows you to communicate with people without using known communication channels. The communication takes place through your mind. If you are a fan of mystical superhero movies, you have likely seen a depiction of telepathy before. It usually involves two or more people talking to each other inside their heads. But the movie depiction of telepathy, as with anything psychic, is somewhat exaggerated. So, don't read this chapter hoping to become Dr. Strange by the time you get to the end.

Telepathy is not a new psychic ability. It has been recorded in different cultures around the globe for hundreds of years. Some sources even say it has been around for as long as five thousand years. Some say it has been around for much longer.

You might feel like this is one psychic ability that is unlikely for you, but you do have the ability. As long as you have psychic senses and portals that allow you to access other psychic abilities, telepathy is just another ability waiting to be accessed. Everyone has the natural, inborn power to communicate through consciousness.

There are four ways telepathy can be used. The first is for reading. Reading means hearing the thoughts running through another person's mind. The second way is for communicating, which is when you interact with another person without using words. The third way is via impressing. This is when you plant a thought, word, or image into the mind of another. Last, you can use telepathy to control when you use it to influence someone else's actions.

Since your consciousness is central to the practice of telepathy, aligning your consciousness with that of another person is the key to communicating telepathically. However, that is not the only way. Energy is also vital to telepathic communication. Every single person has an inherent ability to transmit frequencies through their vibrating energy. When you can align your vibrational frequency with that of another person, you no longer need to communicate with them through the known channels or senses. Aligning your vibrational frequencies establishes a direct link for sending and receiving telepathic messages.

Twin telepathy is one of the most common forms of twin telepathy. Twins are believed to have the "special" ability to interact without speaking or using verbal cues. Suppose you have ever been around any pair of twins. In that case, you might have noticed them finishing each other's sentences or immediately sensing any negative emotion or affect. Many people believe in twin telepathy, yet they don't believe in telepathy among individuals.

Scientific studies have been conducted on twin telepathy. But most of these studies have been based on personal accounts and experiences of some people.

Telepathy comes easily to twins, even when they aren't into esoteric practices because they share the same consciousness grids. They are born on the same vibrational frequency, so they need not struggle to connect telepathically. They already operate on the same wavelength. Also, being born together means that the blueprint for their consciousness grid is similar, almost to where you can't differentiate one from the other without intense scrutiny.

Twin telepathy is proof that telepathy is indeed real and possible. But what are the signs to watch out for should you want to identify telepathy in a person?

You have likely had different telepathic experiences while growing up. At the moment, you may have passed them off as coincidences, but that was your ability showing itself. If you have ever completed someone else's sentences for them, you have had a telepathic experience. Some of the telepathic experiences may have seemed trivial to you at the time. For instance, you might have sensed that your best friend in another state isn't feeling great, called them, and found they weren't. Many people have had several instances like this, but there is a tendency to think of them as coincidences. Some people think of the experiences relative to luck.

A strong intuition always accompanies telepathic ability. The two are not mutually inclusive. If you are telepathic, you are intuitive. To unlock this gift, you have to embrace and trust your intuition. Without trusting your guts, you cannot connect efficiently with other people's vibrations. This makes telepathic communication unattainable.

Another thing about telepathy is that it often occurs when you are in a dream state. Your sleep time is the period where your brain waves at the highest frequency, allowing for a flood of data into your mind. You may believe that time is linear, but it is not. Remember that I said something about the Akashic records and how they contain a collection of every event you have experienced in your past lives. Every thought, feeling, word, and intent from your past, present, and future is contained in the Akashic Records. Therefore, when you dream of something, it is because that thing is happening in real-time in another timeline and dimension.

As a psychic, if you often get intense sensations in the middle of your forehead, that is your third eye itching to unlock your telepathic doorway. Of course, this could also be a sign of another psychic ability. Or it could be a sign of all the psychic abilities lying dormant in your psychic portals. Don't be afraid if you get more of this sensation when you start practicing telepathic techniques. They will subside subsequently.

Telepathy is interconnected with empathy. If you are highly empathetic, then you more than likely have this ability. As you know, empathy involves experiencing other people's feelings almost as real as they experience them. On the other hand, telepathy is linked to thoughts. You can read other people's thoughts inside their heads. If you are clairsentient, both of these abilities are intertwined for you. Being empathetic and telepathic means that your ability goes beyond just thoughts. It extends to feelings as well. I believe that one cannot be a true telepath without empathy.

If you always know when being lied to, that is another pointer to telepathy. Telepaths can sense when the information they are receiving isn't accurate. Usually, you don't even need to look inside someone's head to realize it. You just find you can sense what is going on in their head.

After developing your latent telepathy gifts, you will begin to pick up on thoughts. This is when your clairaudience sense comes to play. You may find you can hear people's thoughts out loud in your head. Sometimes, claircognizance is the psychic sense that comes to the forefront. You start 'knowing' people's thoughts. But the psychic sense involved does not matter. What does matter is that you have access to people's unspoken or unexpressed thoughts.

It does not stop at that. The more practice you put in, the more your ability will advance. You will get to where you can send and receive long-distance messages. You will also be able to plant thoughts, ideas, and messages into others' minds. Naturally, getting to this point requires months or years of practice, depending on how in-tune you are with your psychic side.

## Exercises to Develop Telepathic Abilities

A solid meditation routine and practice is, unsurprisingly, the first thing you must put into practice if you want to develop your telepathic skills. You cannot learn telepathy if your mind is always in a cluttered state. Meditation is for getting rid of any clutter in your mind so you can receive psychic messages. A clear, free, and focused mind is your best chance at linking your consciousness with that of other people.

When you first start practicing, observe, and try to determine your strength. Are you a better sender or receiver? I make a better receiver. Not that one is better than the other, but just as you have a stronger inclination toward one psychic sense, you are also naturally inclined to send or receive more. It helps to practice with what you are better at. Then, you can progress to the opposite once you have learned it to a comfortable level.

An even easier way of determining your preference is to think about the question below.

Are you more likely to call a friend and have them tell you they were just thinking about you? Or are you more likely to think of a friend and unexpectedly receive a call from them?

If you answer yes to the first question, it means you will make a better receiver. But answering yes to the second question tilts you towards a sender.

When you have determined this, you can practice based on your strong suit. If you are naturally inclined towards receiving, start practicing how to receive telepathic messages. In your interactions and conversations with others, put in a deliberate effort to pick up on what they are not saying out loud. Note it does not always come across as words; you might pick up on it in the form of feelings. Try practicing with anyone with which you are comfortable. Tell them to think of something and see if you can determine what it is. Be sure not to do this with a skeptic, as this may cause a vibrational block.

If you tilt more strongly towards sending, practice sending people messages via extrasensory perception. An excellent way of practicing is to meet someone on the street and say "hello" to them normally. But in your mind, think "goodbye" instead. Watch their facial expression as you say and think of two completely different things. If they show any sign of surprise or confusion, it means they received your message. They likely will say nothing to you unless they are familiar with esoteric practices. Still, their nonverbal reaction will be your clue.

Below are two effective exercises for practicing sending and receiving telepathic messages.

### Exercise 1: Tarot Card Technique

To use this technique, you need a willing partner and a deck of tarot cards. You may even use a standard playing deck or an oracle deck if you don't have tarot cards.

- Tell your partner to sit in a specific part of the location far from you. It should be in such a position you can't see each other.

- As the sender or transmitter, draw four cards from the deck and place them on a flat surface. Make sure that they are facing down.

- Next, flip one card over. Relax your mind and concentrate on the card's image, keeping your focus solely on that image. Send the mental image to your partner, who is the receiver. Set the intention for this.

- Your practice partner's job is to try to receive and accept the image you sent and then send it back to you.

- If you want, you can switch positions and act as the receiver instead of the sender.

Trust your gut, and don't second guess yourself.

### Exercise 2: Emotion-Induced Technique

This exercise is to be practiced with someone with whom you already have an established emotional connection. Sending and receiving telepathic messages is much easier when the other party is someone you have an intimate relationship with. This is because the vibrational frequencies are more potent this way. This exercise can be practiced over a long distance, depending on how strong your emotional connection is. The stronger it is, the more they are likely to receive your message regardless of distance.

- Meditate to put yourself in a relaxed and receptive mental state. You shouldn't feel like you are forcing the relaxed state. It should feel as natural as it feels when you have leisure time.

- Make sure that your recipient is also in a relaxed state of mind. If not, they won't be able to receive any message you send. Both of you must enter a receptive and relaxed state before you begin.

- Determine what you want to send and visualize the other person receiving it. With your eyes closed, picture the other person as clearly as you can. Imagine exactly what they are doing at that moment. You may imagine them sitting in front of you. Add all the details that matter, such as the skin tone, eye color, height, weight, hair length, and sitting position. If you are doing it over a distance, look at a picture of them before you start visualizing.
- Build a mental image and visualize it, sending it to the receiver.

Start this technique with a simple word or image. Sticking with something simple helps. For example, you can imagine a banana. Visualize a banana in front of your mind's eye. Focus all your thoughts on the banana and imagine the taste and feel of it as you bite. Don't send the message until you have formed a clear mental image of what you want to send.

Whichever technique you use, be sure to ask your practice partner what they received. This will allow you to know if they did receive your message. If you aren't successful at first, don't let that discourage you. The key to unlocking telepathic skills is to keep practicing until you achieve them. Remember to use a different word, thought, or image for each practice session. As you progress, you can use telepathy to control or influence people's behavior.

# Chapter Eight: Types of Divination

Divination is perhaps the most complex and comprehensive psychic ability. It is the art of finding "hidden" knowledge about the future to interpret it. This is made possible through intuition, divining tools, and the help of Divine power. It is regarded as a branch of magic, but it is also a psychic skill. It's used to foretell the future and determine the significance of an event, supernatural or otherwise. You could say that divination is a way of unraveling destiny.

The art of divination operates on the idea that everything in the universe is connected through energy. We are all connected on an energetic level. Therefore, the whole universe is similar to a massive energy grid that links all of our energy imprints. Once you understand this, it means you can access information from pretty much everything with energy. You need only to find a connector that can link you to the infinite interconnecting grid. Then, you can ask questions and seek answers infinitely.

Many divination practitioners access the infinite energy grid by using divination tools that range from runes, stones, and tarot cards to shells, sticks, and leaves. As the diviner, you can connect to your divination tools to obtain information from the grid and relay them back to yourself or another person through the tool. How clear the information you obtain is depends on your experience, conviction, and ability to clear your mind to ensure clarity when receiving your answers.

Any information that comes from the universal energy grid is a hundred percent accurate. However, it may become distorted or be interpreted inaccurately by the diviner.

Whether you want to use divination for just yourself or you would like to help other people along the way, you can learn different things. Divination can help you determine what is coming your way and when it is coming. It can also guide you when making a decision that could affect your life. Through divining, you get a symbolic message you can only interpret. Usually, a diviner is inspired via a thought, feeling, idea, or memory, then metamorphoses into an answer.

Answers gotten through divination can be subjective. You need real skills to be objective in your interpretation of the information you receive. Otherwise, you may allow your thoughts, feelings, or beliefs to get in the way. A diviner must learn to be objective, nonjudgmental, and devoid of agenda. This is the only way to keep yourself out of the way of the varying energy signatures sent to you from the cosmic wide web.

It is natural for you to have some form of doubt when you first start your divination practice. After all, divination is much more complicated than other psychic practices such as telepathy, mediumship, astral traveling, etc. But you must learn to let go of doubt. Otherwise, it will disturb the clarity of the information. If you have ever been in any divining circle, you have probably heard people say, "Give the message exactly as you receive it." This is to avoid distorting the message.

Always accept the first thing that comes to your mind when you use divination to access the cosmic energy grid. Do not be tempted to change the nuance or nature of what you receive. If you do this, you are bound to let your convictions influence the message's meaning.

Avoid adding any irrelevant or unrelated piece of information or detail to the mix.

Generally, there are several methods of divination. You can't practice all these methods. But you can find one or two that appeal to you and master them. Note that none of the methods is necessarily better than the other. Some people believe that people who use tarot for divination have less talent than people who don't. This is not right.

One reason divination has varying methods is to choose whichever appeals to them the most. If Tarot divination is what you find comfortable, don't be afraid to master it. The divination method you use does not reduce or limit the quality of information you can obtain from the energy grid.

Here, I will be discussing six methods of divination. Since we have discussed Tarots, Pendulums, Runes, and Crystals in an earlier chapter, I won't focus on these. Everything discussed in Chapter three about the use of these psychic tools can be applied to the practice of divination. There is little to no difference since, in the end, the point is to receive psychic messages from a higher source.

The six methods of divination you will be learning are:

- Scrying
- Tea leaves reading
- Sand divination
- Pyromancy
- Osteomancy
- Numerology
- Automatic Writing

One by one, let's expatiate on what these divination methods entail. In this chapter, I will explain each method briefly just to know the basics. The next chapter will go into details on how you can practice some methods.

# Scrying

Scrying is the divination method that involves gazing into water, fire, or crystals. There is also the full-moon scrying, which encompasses the practice of gazing into the full moon whenever there is one. It is one of the oldest methods of divination and has been around for hundreds of years. Some people call it the reflection divination. Throughout history, there have been stories of different people across different cultures staring into mirrors, water, oil, metals, and crystals to read the reflection. The practice of crystal ball reading originated from scrying.

# Tea Leaves Reading

The art of reading tea leaves has been a thing since the 17th century. The technical term is tasseomancy. It has been around for centuries, even before the Dutch brought China tea to Europe. Tasseomancy is a mix of French and Greek. "Tasse" is the French word, and it stands for "cup"; "manteia" is Greek, and it stands for prophecy. So, perhaps the literal translation of tasseomancy is the art of foretelling the future from a cup. Tea isn't the only thing you can use for tasseomancy practice. You may also use wine sediment or coffee grounds. You can tailor your tasseomancy practice to fit your own needs and tastes.

# Sand Divination

Also called geomancy, sand divination is a divination practice that involves reading the shapes of stones and sand for divining purposes. This practice is common with Muslim communities, especially in the Middle East. Geomancy is regarded as one of the most beautiful art forms. Like any other divination form, those who practice sand divination believe in the presence of vital energy in the sand. The "vital energy" in this context is the aura.

# Pyromancy

Many people believe that pyromancy is the oldest divination form. For many centuries, the practice of pyromancy was banned in Europe, alongside hydromancy and necromancy. However, fire is just too fascinating and intriguing to leave alone. Pyromancy is the divining art of gazing into a fire to obtain psychic messages. If you are a fan of the TV show, Game of Thrones, then you should know that the red lady Melissandre was a pyromancy practitioner. Dancing around a fire can help you answer some of the most challenging questions in life.

# Osteomancy

Osteomancy is also called bone divination, and is the art of reading bone for divine information. Osteomancy has been a widespread practice across cultures for thousands of years. Although it has varying applicable techniques, the goal is the same thing – to read messages displayed in the bones. This is one method you may not be able to practice because of the rarity of animal bones. But still, knowing about it may be of benefit to you.

# Numerology

The basics of numerology are that numbers have substantial spiritual significance. It is believed that some numbers are more potent than others. Also, numbers can be combined to foretell the future and make crucial decisions. And numbers are also connected with planetary movements and shifts.

# Automatic Writing

Automatic writing is one of the most known ways to get messages from the spirit world. It is popular among mediums who communicate with ghosts and spirits. It is the same process I described in the chapter about beginning your mediumship. You simply get a pen and paper, relax your mind, and let divine messages flow through you with no conscious effort on your part. Whatever you write down on the paper is channeled from the spirit world.

The next chapter goes more into how you can practice scrying, tea leaves reading, and more of the divination forms discussed in this chapter.

# Chapter Nine: Practice Divination

This chapter will focus on discussing the techniques for practicing the divination forms explained in the preceding chapter. So, let's get to it.

### Scrying

Scrying has long been a method for ancient people to put their wisdom and intuition to use. Everyone knows that water is a very potent source of vital energy. There is a connection to water that we all feel. There is a reason why we feel so energetic after having a warm or cold bath. Your mind and body are intricately linked to water.

The earth, moon, and sky are all water sources, which means that water plays a part in the lunar cycles. You need a clear sky, a full moon, and a bowl of water to practice scrying. Apart from these, you also need a flat surface, a notepad, and meditative music. The last one is, however, optional.

You may decide to cast a circle or not. That depends on you. Play your meditative music to put you in a relaxed state of mind. Gently sit in front of the flat surface where you have a bowl of water. Close your eyes and feel yourself tuning into the energy of your environment. All of your senses should be alert.

Listen as the wind rustles the tree. Smell the scent of leaves around you. Feel the energy wash over you. Focus on gathering the energy you feel. It comes as a sensation that is there for you to feel when you look for it. Feel your connection to that energy and its Divine source. Remain like this for some minutes until you are ready to scry.

When you are ready, open your eyes gently. Observe your environment. You should feel an extraordinary sense of calm, awareness, and clarity. That is due to the energy to which you are attuned. Look at the bowl of water in front of you. Visualize guidance and wisdom swimming within the water. As you visualize, see the energy swirling around the water. Acknowledge that the water can reveal mysteries to you.

Stare into the water and look at the reflection. Search for patterns, pictures, and symbols. Do not take your gaze away from the water. After a while, you will start to see pictures, words, or symbols forming in the reflection on the water. Random thoughts that don't immediately make sense may pop into your head. Take your notepad and write them down exactly as they come. Write everything down.

You may gaze into the water for as long as you want. Spend up to an hour if you wish, but a few minutes is also enough to get the information you seek. Stop when you feel restless or mundane thoughts flood your mind.

When you are done, check to see you wrote down everything that came to you during scrying, including the thoughts, feelings, and sensations. For the next few days, sit on the information and allow your subconscious mind to ruminate on the meaning until it makes sense. Eventually, you can make sense of it all.

If the message you receive doesn't seem to have anything to do with you, think about your loved ones and friends. Try to determine which of them it applies to.

If you have a natural water source near your home, try scrying with larger bowls of water. This makes messages easier to detect amidst all the energy.

**Reading Tea Leaves**

Reading tea leaves is one of the most iconic ways to practice divination. This method may not be as popular as some of the other ones, but it is just as effective. Plus, it is relatively straightforward. You may want to get cups that are designed especially for this divination form. Those cups have symbols and patterns inscribed, allowing for a more straightforward interpretation of any message you receive. So, how exactly does one read tea leaves?

First, you will need a cup of tea to begin. The tea has to contain all the leaves, so don't use a strainer when brewing. Using a strainer will get rid of all the leaves, and there will be nothing to read. Your teacup should be light-colored to allow you to see whatever is happening to the leaves inside the cup.

The larger the leaves of the tea, the more accurate your reading will be. So, take note of this when making the tea. Use a loose tea leaf blend, so the leaves don't become too small. Go for blends like Earl Grey because they usually have large leaves. After making the tea, consume it at your own pace.

After this, all you will have left at the bottom of your teacup are leaves. Firmly shake the cup so the leaves can form a pattern. One way to do this is to swirl the cup around in a circle a couple of times. Do it three times to avoid having wet leaves around.

Next, observe the leaves and see if you can see any images in the patterns they form. This is where you start divination. Typically, diviners interpret the images in two ways. The first way is to follow a standard set of symbols passed down from century to century. For example, if you get an image that appears like a dog, it means you have a loyal friend in your corner. An apple represents education or knowledge. You can get material with information on tea leaf symbols and their interpretation. While you may find variations in the interpretations, the meanings are pretty much universal.

The second way is to use your intuition to interpret the leaves' images that appear to you. Concentrate on how the images make you feel and think. The image may be that of a dog, but it may not inspire a positive feeling symbolic of a loyal friend to you. Here, you have to trust your intuition. Intuitive interpretation requires you to trust your instinct.

Multiple images may also appear to you. When this happens, read the images starting from your teacup's handle, and go around clockwise. If the cup has no handle, start from the very top, the farthest away from you.

Don't forget to have your notepad with you as you do the reading. Whenever you practice, keep the notepad handy. This will allow you to go back to the things that appear to you in the teacup.

### Numerology

The basis of numerology is the belief that numbers have powerful spiritual and magical significance. In some numerology variants, it is believed that odd numbers are feminine energy numbers. In contrast, even numbers have masculine energy and meaning. Universally, each culture has a different interpretation of what the numbers mean.

In some traditions, the meanings of numbers include:

> 1: Linked to the cosmic life force that connects everyone in the universe. It is regarded as a source and a grounding number. Using tarot cards, 1 symbolizes a person who takes control of his environment and achieves personal power by taking advantage of the people around him.

> 2: This symbolized duality and polarity. It is the number of balances. When you think of the number 2, think of yin and yang, light and dark, and other opposites. This number represents one of each thing,

3: In many numerology traditions, 3 is considered the most magical of all the numbers. It is symbolic of the realms of the sky, sea, and land. It also represents your mental, physical, and spiritual needs. Three also symbolizes action and interaction. In other traditions, it is the number for neutrality and passiveness.

4: Connects to all the four elements – fire, earth, water, and air. It also represents the four seasons and the four cardinal directions of the world. It is also a symbol of creativity.

5: Five is the number of spirits. It is symbolic of your five human senses. It is regarded as a symbol of chaos, struggle, and conflict in some traditions.

6: Represents solar energy. It is a vital source of masculine energy. It represents responsibility and security.

7: Represents lunar energy. It is connected to the moon and femininity. This number is symbolic of intuition and wisdom, representing consciousness and thought-forms.

8: Eight is associated with the planet mercury, which concerns communication and messages. It is an infinity symbol when flipped on its side.

9: Three times three is nine, which makes nine a triply potent number. It is linked with goddess energy. Nine indicates growth and change. Using the tarot represents the completion of a new process.

0: Zero represents nothing. It represents the potential you have to create something new out of nothing. Zero is a sign of the beginning.

Check through tarot divination, pendulum divination, crystal divination, and all the other divination forms we have just discussed, and choose the one you think will work best for you.

# Chapter Ten: The Power of Clairvoyance

Clairvoyance is the most popular psychic sense in most psychics. Some of us have clairvoyance as our dominant psychic sense, coupled with another psychic sense. If you remember clearly, we briefly discussed its basics in chapter two. You have already learned that clairvoyance means "clear seeing." It is the psychic ability to see and read energy. Since we have already talked about its meaning and what it entails, this chapter will focus wholly on how you can hone and develop your 6th sense to sharpen your clairvoyance sense.

Clairvoyance is the one psychic sense common to all the psychic abilities we have discussed so far in this book. If you successfully hone this sense, you will find that any psychic ability you want to learn becomes easier when your clairvoyance is awakened. The key to developing your clairvoyance is to awaken your third eye. Therefore, below are six exercises you can use to awaken your third eye and open up the pathway to clairvoyance.

### 1. Visualization

This is one of the best ways to strengthen your third eye and intuition. There are so many ways you can practice visualization. One of these is flower visualization. Getting started is easy. Buy a flower that looks pretty and smells good. Place the flower before you and observe it for some minutes. After this, close your eyes and picture the flower with as many details as possible. Imagine the shape, size, color, and all other details.

Another visualization exercise is to imagine the number one in your mind's eye. Envision that you see the number one. Make it as big as you want with whatever colors you want. You can even imagine some sprinkle of glitter. Hold this image in your third eye for at least 10 seconds. Next, open your eyes and do a quick breathing exercise.

Repeat these steps from number one to two, three, etc., until you get to 10.

## 2. Talk to Your Spirit Guides

Talking to your spirit guides is another way you can develop your clairvoyance ability. Suppose you interact with your spirit guides regularly. In that case, you can ask them to send you messages in the form of beautiful images. If you have never met your spirit guides, don't fret. Use the meditation technique discussed and call out to your spirit guide to talk to you. Then, wait for their message to appear to you. Don't forget that the message can take different forms. It may come as images, words, thoughts, feelings, or physical sensations.

## 3. Play Clairvoyant Games

There is a game we used to play when we were younger. The game is called **Memory**. If you played the game when you were younger, you might remember that you used to place cards face down, flip one over at a time, trying to make a match. This game can sharpen your third eye and increase clairvoyance. Before you flip each card over, use your mind eye to try to "see" which card is which.

Another fun game for clairvoyance is to have someone place ten random objects on your table. Don't stay in the room while the person is setting up the items. Now, close your eyes and visualize each object. Try using your third eye to "see" where each item is located and its color and size. Write down details about each item. Be as specific as possible about the items. When you are done writing, open your eyes. Go to where the items are and see how accurate you were.

You can practice this particular exercise alone. Go to your nearest part, study the environment, then close your eyes and visualize as many details as possible about your surroundings.

### 4. Practice Aura Reading

Aura is your human energy field, as I have established. It is in the form of lights and colors. Anyone can train themselves to see this energy around all living things. This makes it an excellent exercise for building clairvoyance. To practice seeing auras, you need a practice partner. Ask the person to stand in front of a white-colored wall or any other plain-looking wall. Step back some feet until you reach a point where you can see your partner's head and shoes without looking up or down. Concentrate and look through the person to the wall behind them. Focus and the outline of the aura will start appearing around their head.

### 5. Journal

Journals are a critical part of any psychic development journey. Before you start your journey, get a journal to record all your spiritual and psychic experiences. Any time you connect with Spirit and your Higher Self or even have a meaningful dream, write everything down. By doing this, you can connect more with your intuition and your clairvoyance sense to make sense of the messages you receive.

### 6. Awaken Your Third Eye

Open your third eye through third eye chakra meditation. The purpose of the third eye meditation is to help you improve mental clarity, focus the mind, and increase concentration. The meditation is brief and straightforward.

Sit comfortably in a chair. Make your spine upright, and your shoulder relaxed. Your chest should be open. Place your hands on your knees with the palms facing upward. Gently touch your index finger to your thumb. Relax your body from the face to the jaw and belly. Your tongue should rest behind your front teeth, and your eyes should be lightly closed.

Breathe in and out through your nose. Do this deeply and smoothly. With your eyes still closed, look up at the area of your forehead. This is where you have your third eye chakra. Concentrate your gaze on this spot intently. Wait until a bright purple or indigo color appears. Gently take your mind away from thoughts in your mind and maintain your focus on the third eye.

Remain in this position for at least 10 minutes while breathing in and out gently and deeply. After your ten minutes are up, inhale and exhale gently, pull your palms together and bring them both to the front of your heart. Then, end the meditation with these words, "May the Divine grant me the ability to see and perceive the truth clearly on every level." Round up and gently open your eyes before going back to your daily business.

You can do the third eye meditation every day if you want your third eye to open up quickly. However, when you start getting uncomfortable sensations in the spot where your third eye is, stop the meditation, or your third eye will open up completely and become overactive. An overactive third eye does more harm than good to psychics.

When the third eye becomes overactive, you will no longer have control over your thoughts and feelings. You might become susceptible to an influx of psychic messages, all of which will be too much to handle. So, be careful when opening your third eye.

# Chapter Eleven: Spiritual Healing: Work with Energy

Energy healing is the psychic and holistic practice of activating your subtle energy bodies to eliminate blocks and create a passage for energy to flow freely. By getting rid of the energy block, your body's innate ability to heal itself of physical, mental, and emotional conditions is activated. In an earlier chapter, I talked about how blockage in the subtle bodies can disrupt energy flow through the body system, resulting in imbalance. This results in illnesses and diseases of the body and mind.

The point of energy healing is to take a holistic approach towards restoring the balance in energy flow through your body, mind, and spirit. Energy healing directly affects the physical, mental, emotional, and spiritual aspects of your wellbeing. Energy healers have mastered the art of using energy to treat various medical conditions, particularly those that concern your mental health.

They do this by using vital energy to determine the root of the disturbance in the energy system. Once they locate the spot of the blockage, the flow of energy is restored. The ill person automatically becomes cured when the flow disruption is fixed. To heal with energy, you first need to master your energy body. Please refer to Chapter

Four. Once you have mastered your energy field and astral form, you can use your energy to heal other people's energy systems.

Energy disruption is often caused by an accumulation of physical, mental, and emotional stress. It may also be caused by environmental stress, trauma, and negative belief systems. These are factors that act as blocks to your spiritual and personal growth. They often accumulate and store in your energy field, resulting in decreased functions.

Using energy healing techniques, you can facilitate the healing process to eliminate blocks in your field, repair and restore the balance of the chakras, and more important, repurpose energy around your body so it can return to an optimal state of functioning. From there, the body can gain back its ability to heal itself.

Besides this, energy healing techniques can also help you find and identify problems before they manifest physically as pain or distortion. Learning energy healing opens up your consciousness to whatever part of your body requires or needs healing. Doing this helps bring a sense of harmony, health, and vitality to your life.

There are different energy healing techniques. To become an energy healer, you have to master some of these techniques. Some of the most popular techniques explicitly used to heal energy are Reiki and Acupuncture. Besides these, you also have lesser-known techniques such as Chakra balancing, Spiritual healing, and Crystal Healing. The subsequent chapter focuses on crystal healing practice, so I won't be touching on that here. Remember that I have also explained chakra balancing in a previous chapter. Therefore, we won't be talking about that.

# Reiki Healing

Reiki was created over a hundred years ago by Mikao Usui, a Japanese Buddhist. It is a healing therapy founded on the principle we are all guided by an invisible life force (Energy) that controls our physical, emotional, and mental wellbeing. When this life force flows freely without restriction, we can access unknown power reserves across the universe. When the life force is exposed to blockage, which is often caused by an overload of stress, trauma, or negative thoughts, it affects our system's functionality. This is the same thing I explained in the chapter where you learned about the energy body.

Someone who isn't well-versed with spiritual practices may easily discard this as magic or voodoo. Still, many nonspiritual people have attested to the efficacy of Reiki in treating physical and mental conditions. Most people who have witnessed the awesomeness of Reiki healing have reported feeling a huge positive shift in countenance, thinking, and overall vibes. Reiki is a mix of energy sweeping and light touches all over the body. It may feel like grounding for some people while, for others, it feels like emotional realignment.

The first step in any Reiki healing is to receive energy. Start by activating your energy source within your system. Close your eyes and run through a few rounds of powerful and deep breathing. Visualize your crown chakra opening up with a stream of white light flowing out. The white light is healing. Picture the light moving from the top of your head into your chakra, to your arms and hands. Ask that the light fills up the part of your body where you require the most healing.

As the energy flows from one part of your body to the next, keep breathing. Do this until the energy has touched every part of your body where you need healing. Your mind might get busy along the line. Simply bring your focus back to the sensation of your breathing as you continue. Imagine yourself as a medium for healing. Pray to the Divine so you can receive healing of the greatest quality. If you use

Reiki healing to help a loved one, you have to make sure you are filled with energy first.

Reiki can help another person improve their sleep. To do this, follow the steps below.

- Ask the loved one or recipient to lie down flat on the bed while you hover around their head. Visualize a bright stream of light emerging from your hand into their system through the back of their head. Set an intention for the light to clear their mind of any discomfort building up.

- Tell the recipient to breathe in and out in several rounds. Ask them to visualize their whole memory from the day at once and show appreciation for the memory. Then, ask them to release the memory with their breath.

- Continue to channel the healing light from your hands into their energy field. Ask them to picture their body healing, relaxing, and getting heavy for a pleasant night's sleep.

Fifteen to thirty minutes is enough to practice Reiki for sleep on your loved one or any other person you wish to try it on. By the time you are done, they should be relaxed and calm enough to drift off to sleep.

Reiki may also relieve stress and anxiety, which are some things that result in energy blockage in the system. Stress and anxiety disrupt a person's breathing, resulting in shortness of breath. This also causes more stress.

Reiki's purpose for stress is to channel energy into the recipient's body to eliminate tension and release the knotted nerves.

- Place your palms on the person's shoulders for up to 15 minutes.

- Send the pure energy from your hand into their body.

- Breathe deeply and ask them to breathe with you. Let your breathing sync. This will naturally release some of the tense mental energy into their body.
- If the person is lying flat, put your hand behind their head to help them calm down and relax.

For as much relaxation as possible, keep this technique going for about 15 or 20 minutes.

To conclude, you have to seal off the energy from your crown. Offer your gratitude for the successful healing process. Cleanse yourself with the energy from your hand. Then, close the source of energy to complete the healing session. You may do something as simple as wiping your hands of excess energy and releasing that remaining in prayer. End the sessions with both of your hands raised in prayer.

# Qigong

Qigong is a spiritual healing therapy used to restore the body's lost balance. This technique has existed for as far back as 4000 years. It comprises a series of coordinated body movements, which include breathing and meditation. The point of Qigong is to stimulate healthy, vitality, and spirituality in your body, mind, and soul. From the name, you can already tell this healing therapy works with energy. Qi is Chinese for energy.

This healing technique involves moving energy through the channels and centers while fixing the flow, strengthening it, and balancing it across the different energy points throughout your whole body. Its exercises can prevent illnesses, heal them, maintain quality health, and increase one's chances of longevity. One thing about this energy healing thing is that you can use it for anybody across any age. Your physical condition does not matter. Qigong can significantly benefit the quality of your overall health.

There are some basic Qigong exercise techniques.

The first is concentration. This is a technique that is geared towards increasing energy awareness. It has to do with learning how to focus and let go simultaneously. In other words, Qigong concentration helps you master how to accommodate your mind, body, and spirit's functions while being focused and undistracted by extraneous factors. In doing this, you allow the worries of your everyday hassles to drift away.

Breathing is also a Qigong exercise technique. The technique is targeted at stimulating vital energy with your breaths. The two most common breathing methods to fill your body with energy are Buddha's Breath and Daoist's breath.

Buddha's breath requires you to inhale and expand your belly with air. When you finally exhale, contract your belly and release the breath, starting from the bottom area of your lungs and pushing it out until the air deflates from your tummy and chest. As you inhale and exhale, visualize your Qi flowing through the energy channels. Using your mind, allow it to flow in an orderly way. Don't tug or push at the energy.

Daoist's breath is the direct opposite of Buddha's breath. You can repeat the steps stated above but do it in contrast. Breathe in and contract your belly muscles. Then, exhale and allow your torso and lungs to relax.

As you go through these steps, never forget that Qigong is an ongoing way of increasing awareness at the highest level. Still, don't practice unless you are comfortable. Do the exercises you find comfortable.

Below is a quick Qigong awareness exercise:

- Shut your eyes halfway. Clear the clutter in your mind and focus on your palms.

- Breathe slowly and gently, without force. You should feel like you are inducing a trance.

- Draw your hands together, with the palms touching and your fingers pointed upward. Make sure the centers of your palms touch each other. That way, you can feel when energy starts emanating from your body.

- Slowly move your hands apart until they are around 12 inches away from each other. It should feel like you are compressing air between your hands.

- You will start feeling a tingling sensation in the spot where the palms are touching.

- Start a back-and-forth movement of your hands. Let the range of the bellows vary.

This exercise can help channel energy, build awareness, and enlighten yourself. Prepare for a mindset change when you experience the powers of Qi energy for the first time.

# Pranic Healing

The Indian word for Energy is Prana. Therefore, Pranic healing is just another way of saying energy healing. It is a form of healing technique in which prana, also known as the universal life force, is heightened, controlled, and used for specific healing purposes and benefits. Pranic healing can be used for yourself or the people around you, and the process entails projecting prana from a pure source into the system of people who need healing. There are different levels of pranic healing.

First, you have basic Pranic healing. It is the most basic healing level, which involves projecting your prana energy into a person's body. It further entails scanning the person's body, cleaning, balancing, and letting go of the projected energy. The healer, who is you, also has to cut off the energy cord between the energy receiver and themselves. This is to prevent contamination and speed the healing process up.

Second, you have advanced Pranic healing, when you master how to use prana energy to purge and purify a person's body to invigorate and revitalize them.

Third, Pranic psychotherapy involves mastering the ability to use colorful prana energy to cure mental illnesses and psychological disorders.

The fourth and final is the Pranic crystal healing, which revolves around using healing crystals to focus energy on someone on a more intense level.

Naturally, you have to start at the basic level. As you practice more, you can progress to other levels of pranic healing.

Here, I have the procedure involved in performing basic pranic healing meditation. It involves seven steps, all of which must be followed in order.

- Step 1: Cleansing is the first step in pranic healing. You start by performing a couple of simple exercises for purifying the energy body. The purpose of cleansing is to get rid of any accumulated energy congestion in the auric field.

- Step 2: Invocation is the second step in pranic healing. It is significant in this meditation. You simply have to seek divine blessings and guidance in your meditation. This is to make sure you have absolute protection and appropriate help during the procedure.

- Step 3: The third step is the activation of the third chakra. Do this by pressing two fingers to the area where your heart is located. Visualize and focus on your heart chakra. Imagine the earth as a little glowing ball with shining bluish-pink light and use it to bless everyone across the universe. Visualize everyone on Earth, including yourself, being filled with wonderful feelings of peace, delight, hope, and devotion.

- Step 4: The next step is the activation of the Crown chakra. Just as you did in step 3, press two fingers to the top of your head where your crown is located. Wait for a couple of seconds while focusing on the crown chakra. Send blessings to everyone across the planet and ask that they are filled with love, light, and kindness. Feel the positive flow of energy pumping through your own body and mind.

- Step 5: Envision a shining white light emerging from your crown chakra. Imagine the light flooding the entire planet. This means you are blessing the whole earth with the white light from your crown chakra and golden light from your heart chakra. This will make your blessing more plentiful and potent. Again, feel the positive flow of energy as it runs through your mind and body.

- Step 6: The sixth step is the stage where you achieve illumination, basically expanding awareness. Imagine the radiant white light on your crown chakra and chant "OM" and "Amen" together. Do this for up to 15 minutes. Chant the mantra and focus on the light simultaneously. Once it gets to a point, you will feel light explode within you.

- Step 7: The final step involves releasing the remnant energy inside you. It is the perfect closing to your meditation. Use some more additional minutes to bless the earth while allowing the energy to be released through your hand into the earth.

Before you round up your session, allow your body to return to its normal, stable self. Otherwise, you may experience a series of acute chest pain and migraine.

# Quantum Healing

Quantum healing entails using a combination of breathing and visualization exercises to increase the energy level in your system. Quantum healing not only has spiritual benefits but also has a direct medical impact on your immune system. Essentially, quantum healing combines meditation and Eastern medicine with mind-body medicine and quantum physics. By shifting the vital life force at a quantum level, you can use quantum healing techniques to heal your mind, body, and spirit.

I don't advise beginners to try quantum healing on their own unless they have taken a comprehensive course to prepare themselves. So, this is not to tell you to try quantum healing by yourself. Still, there are body awareness exercises related to this technique. They are brief and straightforward, so you can try them on your own.

The core principle of quantum healing is to raise your vibrational levels using resonance and entrainment. Therefore, body awareness and breathing techniques are a good start for anyone interested in quantum healing.

Here are some exercises to try.

- **Feeling Your Finger:** Hold out your middle finger. Pay attention and be aware of the finger. Don't take your focus away from it. In the next few minutes, you will notice a tingling sensation, buzzing, heat, heaviness, and vibration in that finger. Your awareness of the finger becomes increased.

- **1-4 Breath:** Deeply and completely breathe in to the count of one and breathe out to the count of four. Do this until you start feeling dizzy. Then, stop.

- **4-4 Breathe:** Mentally do a body sweep from your feet to your crown as you breathe in to the count of four. Take one second for each count. You should start to feel waves of sensations as you bring awareness from one part of your body to the next. Breathe out to the count of four and allow all generated sensations to concentrate in your hands.

As with all the psychic abilities we have discussed so far, you have to put in practice if you want to learn all these energy healing techniques.

# Chapter Twelve: Crystals for Healing and Personal Power

As you progress in your psychic journey, there are certain things you must make a constant. Crystals are part of things that can increase your psychic abilities and enhance your healing power. They are not just beautiful. They also have a lot of properties that make them a must-have. Crystals are packed with a lot of energy to bestow their owners with clarity, protection, and guidance. Other than this, you can also use them to amplify your psychic abilities.

For centuries, crystals have been used in various ways due to their powerful properties. Their powerful energy allows them to have an easy impact on the body and mind. Due to their connection with the cosmos and yourself, they are the best tools to have in your psychic development journey. Some people think that crystals are an outdated way of connecting with the spirit world. These people have no idea what they are missing out on. Forget how crystals are portrayed and used in Hollywood movies and focus on reality.

Crystals are natural minerals from the bottom of the earth. Their connection with the earth is likely why they have such potent energetic properties.

Choosing crystals for your personal use depends absolutely on what you want to use them for. But the coolest thing about them is that you don't have to choose them. They choose you. A crystal's powerful energy can connect with your own and draw you to them. When you go crystal shopping, you will just find yourself compelled to pick a particular crystal. If this happens to you, be sure to choose that crystal. Never forget that your intuition is more aware than you can fully comprehend.

Below, I will list the best crystals you can use to increase your psychic senses. But before that, there are a few things to remember. First, when you go through the crystal list, observe the ones that seem more interesting to you. Don't overanalyze; just notice which ones draw you in. There's no definitive guide to picking the right crystal. Just allow yourself to have fun.

If you go to pick out crystals in person, hold and feel them in your hands. See how they make you feel. You are bound to notice differences in how each crystal makes you feel. If you are buying the crystals online, breathe deeply, and center yourself. As you browse through the pictures online, ask yourself how they make you feel.

With this in mind, you can pick your crystals. All crystals are energetic items. They all have the power to open up your body and mind to your inherent psychic abilities. But some crystals have more powerful energies than others. Here are some of the most potent crystals for increasing your psychic abilities.

- **Amethyst:** This is a gorgeous purple stone that is incredibly powerful, purifying, and healing. Amethyst is good for third eye development. It can be used to get rid of negative and toxic energy. It also cleanses the blood, boosts hormone production, and relieves stress and anxiety. It is also said to help promote sobriety and improve a person's sleeping situation.

- **Azurite:** This is another favorite for the third eye. Azurite vibrates at the same level as the third eye, meaning it is suitable for anyone looking to hone their psychic gifts, such as clairvoyance.
- **Clear Quartz:** This is a white crystal that many psychics consider a master healer. Clear quartz crystal is said to can absorb, store, release, and amplify energy. It also has the natural ability to improve focus and concentration. It can also cleanse and balance the immune system by stimulating it. You may pair this stone with other stones to amplify its energy and abilities. A good pairing is with the rose quartz crystal.
- **Rose Quartz:** This pink stone is a symbol of love. It is used to maintain harmony and trust in one's relationships. To improve your relationship and intimate connections, this is the stone to go for. It can also help build love, trust, respect, and worth.
- **Bloodstone:** Another brilliant stone for developing your psychic abilities. Feeling grounded is essential in your journey, and this is what bloodstone can help you achieve. This stone is also great for activating the root chakra. Don't forget that the root chakra is your key to staying grounded in Mother Earth. Place a grid of this crystal under your bed before you sleep and notice the difference.
- **Obsidian:** This is a very powerful stone for protecting yourself from physical, mental, and emotional toxicity. You can use it to get rid of emotional blockages in the energy system. It also helps with the detoxification of the physical body.

Each crystal has different vibrations. It does not even matter if they are of the same stone variation. Using crystals for healing and increasing your psychic ability is a way of receiving multiple benefits in one go.

Caring for your crystal is important. Cleanse your crystals regularly to ward off negativity and toxicity. You can rinse them with warm or cold water. You may also do the cleansing with sea salt or by burning sage.

The most important thing is to accept and respect what your crystals can do for you. Follow all the tips, and your psychic journey will be a smooth and seamless one.

# Conclusion

Psychic development can either be a fascinating and enlightening journey if you approach it the right way. Like I said, psychic skills cannot be learned in one go. You have to put in months and years of consistent practice if you want to make progress. Be careful as your journey the world of mediums and psychics. If possible, find a mentor that can make the whole journey much more enduring and fun for you. If you don't allow yourself to have fun along the way, you may end up halting your learning abruptly. Find ways to make sure this does not happen. A genuine psychic always follows through to the end no matter how tough.

More importantly, don't forget to never compare your progress with that of another person around you. Good luck!

# Here's another book by Mari Silva that you might like

## Your Free Gift (only available for a limited time)

Thanks for getting this book! If you want to learn more about various spirituality topics, then join Mari Silva's community and get a free guided meditation MP3 for awakening your third eye. This guided meditation mp3 is designed to open and strengthen ones third eye so you can experience a higher state of consciousness. Simply visit the link below the image to get started.

https://spiritualityspot.com/meditation

# References

Mediumship - New World Encyclopedia. (n.d.). Www.Newworldencyclopedia.org.

https://www.newworldencyclopedia.org/entry/Mediumship

(PDF) Telepathy: Evidence and New Physics. (n.d.). ResearchGate.

https://www.researchgate.net/publication/323811942_Telepathy_Evidence_and_New_Physics

Psychic Readings | Tarot Reading | Psychics.com. (n.d.). Www.Psychics.com.

The Editors of Encyclopedia Britannica. (n.d.). Clairvoyance | psychology. Encyclopedia Britannica. https://www.britannica.com/topic/clairvoyance

Printed in Great Britain
by Amazon